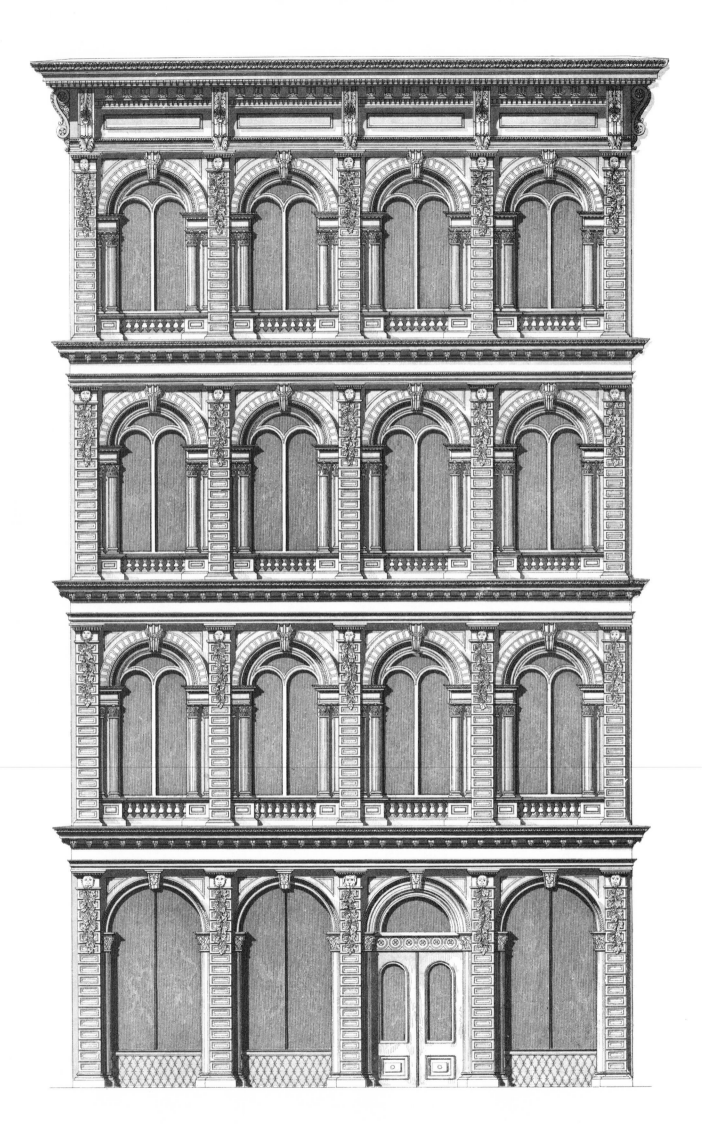

Badger's Illustrated Catalogue of
CAST-IRON ARCHITECTURE

by
Daniel D. Badger

(The Architectural Iron Works of the City of New York)

With a New Introduction by
MARGOT GAYLE

President, Friends of Cast-Iron Architecture

DOVER PUBLICATIONS, INC.
NEW YORK

Margot Gayle is president of the Friends of Cast Iron Architecture, a national organization established in 1970 to arouse interest in our heritage of iron architecture with the goal of preserving what survives. The author of many articles and three books, *Cast-Iron Architecture in New York* (Dover 22980-7), *Victorian Ironwork* and *Metals in America's Historic Buildings,* Mrs. Gayle has lectured at many museums and universities. She is a member of the Art Commission of the City of New York.

Copyright © 1981 by Dover Publications, Inc.
All rights reserved under Pan American and International Copyright Conventions.

Published in Canada by General Publishing Company, Ltd., 30 Lesmill Road, Don Mills, Toronto, Ontario.
Published in the United Kingdom by Constable and Company, Ltd.

This Dover edition, first published in 1981, is an unabridged republication of the work first published by Baker & Godwin, Printers, New York, in 1865 under the title *Illustrations of Iron Architecture Made by The Architectural Iron Works of the City of New York.* An introduction has been written by Margot Gayle specially for the Dover edition.

International Standard Book Number: 0-486-24223-4
Library of Congress Catalog Card Number: 81-68875

Manufactured in the United States of America
Dover Publications, Inc.
180 Varick Street
New York, N.Y. 10014

Introduction to the Dover Edition
by Margot Gayle

Illustrations of Iron Architecture, the 1865 catalogue of Daniel D. Badger's Architectural Iron Works of New York, is a classic—unquestionably the most important volume of its type published in this country. Widely used by architectural historians and other scholars, it is a primary source documenting iron architecture in America.

What is Cast-iron Architecture?

Through the centuries structures have been made by man from wood, stone or clay in the form of bricks, adobe or concrete, but the use of metal was limited to decorative devices such as railings or panels or fasteners such as nails, hinges, straps, anchors or tie rods.

Cast iron, the highest carbon alloy of iron, had been used in ancient China for certain religious objects. Later, in medieval Europe, occasional iron grave slabs were cast and small items were produced that had to withstand heat, such as kettles, trivets, firebacks and firedogs. However, cast iron was not available in any great quantity until the eighteenth century, when advances in raising the heat in furnaces to a point where the melted iron would flow into molds made possible the production of cast iron on a large scale.

Slowly at first, iron began to be cast into sizable forms useful for structural purposes, the most dramatic of which were ribs for the cast-iron bridges in England. The very first of these was the iron bridge, still in use, at Coalbrookdale, put in place over the Severn River in 1789. Not long after, slender cast-iron pillars, cruciform in section, were cast to replace wooden columns in textile mills where intense efforts were being made to render the buildings less vulnerable to fire. We can still see these pillars in Charles Bage's 1797 Shrewsbury flax mill, combined with iron beams supporting brick arches that carry the floors. It is the prototype of the iron-framed building that would become more and more sophisticated during the course of the nineteenth century. By mid-century, wrought-iron beams could be imported into this country from England; in 1853 they were first rolled successfully in the United States by Peter Cooper at Trenton.

The perfect marriage was that of cast-iron columns, tremendously strong in compression, with wrought-iron spanning members or girders, the wrought-iron being strong in tension. Although cast iron and wrought iron are close relatives as ferrous metals, they are very different. Cast iron, rich in carbon, can be put into a molten state and formed, in a mold, into a shape that it will hold until remelted. Wrought iron, with very little carbon but an intermix of glassy slag, can be heated into a spongy mass which then must be shaped by hammering on a forge or by rolling under great pressure. So vigorous was the use of the two materials in combination that it made possible metal-frame structures many stories tall, some of which, including several famous early high-rise buildings in Chicago, can still be seen. One is the famous 1886 Rookery, another the 16-story Manhattan Building, built in 1890 and for a time the world's tallest building. Both still stand.

William Fairburn, noted English engineer, devised not an iron skeleton but an all-iron building to serve as a flour mill in Turkey. Along with the iron bridges of England, it inspired James Bogardus, a versatile New York inventor, when he saw it on exhibit in London. Bogardus returned to the United States and devised his own version of iron buildings. He worked out a system of individually cast iron architectural parts—columns, lintels and panels—that could be bolted together to form a freestanding building with walls, roof and floors. He received a patent for his method of fastening the parts together and went on to plan the casting of iron parts to be put together to form a facade only, perhaps several stories tall, to be assembled and raised onto a conventional structure with rear and side walls of brick and floors of wood. To demonstrate the system, he exhibited a model of the iron factory intended for his own use and finally, in 1849, built it on the northeast corner of Duane and Centre Streets.

Before he could complete his factory, Bogardus was importuned to create iron fronts for two commercial buildings in downtown New York. They were described in the press in 1848 and 1849 and must have riveted the attention of iron founders whose stock in trade was stoves and furnaces or pipes, safes, rolling iron shutters or parts for machinery. Among these foundries were Janes, Beebe Co.; James L. Jackson; J. B. & W. W. Cornell; and Daniel D. Badger, all of whom were soon retooling to produce, along with their regular products, the iron parts for building construction. A whole new market for iron castings had been opened up by James Bogardus.

Bogardus himself never operated a foundry. Styling himself architect, or engineer, or eccentric-mill maker, he contracted out the iron work he required. Thus he was not a foundry man and as such, as some claim, a rival of Badger.

Bogardus erected the big iron fronts for the new Sun Newspaper Building in Baltimore. Work got under way on the impressive structure early in 1851. It stood on a corner and had two facades of iron ornamented along the top story with statues. Bogardus and the New York architect R. C. Hatfield were associated on the project, and Bogardus brought in Badger to supply the ground-floor iron storefront columns fitted with his patent rolling shutters, described below.

After the Harper publishing plant in New York suffered a disastrous fire in 1853, the Harper brothers called on Bogardus to build an iron-front building with every fireproof feature possible. He designed his version of a bowstring girder, which the James L. Jackson foundry produced for him, and used scores of these to span between ornamented cast-iron columns. Then, spanning between these girders, brick jack arches were built to support the concrete floors. The 200-foot iron front had the same design, statues and all, as that created for the Sun Building. It stood just south of where pylons for the Brooklyn Bridge approach were constructed a quarter of a century later. In the early 1850s Bogardus also built multistoried iron-frame fire lookout

towers and the iron-frame McCullough shot tower. These, especially
the shot tower, with its curtain walls of brick infill, held within their
system of construction the seed of the skeleton-framed skyscraper. By
1856 Bogardus had written his celebrated pamphlet entitled "Cast-Iron
Buildings: Their Construction and Advantages" and stated in it that he
had shipped iron architecture to Washington, Baltimore, Charleston
and San Francisco, and by 1858 to Philadelphia, Chicago and Havana,
Cuba.

The iron fronts which would constitute one or more exterior walls
of a building were composed of a multiplicity of parts, each cast
separately in a sand mold. For each section a wooden pattern was
carved. Sometimes these patterns were themselves works of art, the
pride of the elite class of the foundry world, the patternmakers. A
patternmaker's knowledge of proportion, of ornament, of degree of
shrinkage of the metal as it cooled, and of "draw" of the pattern from
the fragile sand mold, was a nice blend of instinct and experience.

Once the pattern, usually of wood, was made, countless impres-
sions rammed into the moist, or "green," sand could be made from it,
and identical iron elements could be turned out by the score or hundred
if need be. Industrially produced architecture had arrived with this
mass production of identical interchangeable elements.

After being machined to assure levelness and polished to a final
smoothness and a perfect fit, the smaller parts were bolted together at
the foundry. Then the entire front was laid out piece by piece on the
floor of the foundry so that all parts could be accounted for, numbered
and checked for fit. After a coat of primer paint was applied, the parts
were ready for shipment to the building site. If the site was a few blocks
away, the iron was carefully wrapped, piled on wagons and then
trundled along by heavy dray horses; if the site was in another town,
the parts were crated and sent by railroad, or even by ship, in some in-
stances around the Horn of South America to the West Coast.

The stylish ornament that cast iron offered was part of its great ap-
peal for architectural purposes in the Victorian age. Ornaments of all
kinds could be molded at moderate cost to give structures a luxurious
mien. Columns, cornices, pediments, keystones and balustrades—not
to mention swags, wreaths, flutings and dentils—would cost a princely
sum if carved in stone or, as was sometimes done, in wood to simulate
stone. The same elements and details, cast in iron and painted, gave
much the same effect as stone. In fact, where other materials weathered
and deteriorated, iron was a remarkably strong and resistant material
that could quickly be freshened with a new coat of paint.

Iron offered more substantive advantages. In comparison with
stone and brick it was stronger and lighter. Less material was needed to
do the same job. A slender iron column could support a weight that
otherwise would require a bulky stone pier or an entire brick wall. An
iron-front building often actually had a dainty look due to the delicacy
of the elements. Such is the case with the pretty little two-story front
seen in Badger's catalogue on Plate XXXVII, No. 18. A person with
an experienced eye can usually distinguish an iron front from its stone
neighbor by this very delicacy of elements which has as its corollary a
wide expanse of glass. For with less wall surface there can be more window surfaces.

This brings us to an important advantage of iron structures in the
days before the versatile electric artificial lighting to which we are now
so accustomed. Most buildings built in rows along urban streets receive
light only through windows in front and back walls. The interior of a
modest business establishment in New York City, for example, built to
cover its standard 25-x-100-foot lot, would enjoy very little natural
light. Even in daytime the occupants would have to rely on flickering
gas jets. The windows could not be large in a masonry front, or the wall
would be weakened, but with an iron front they could be much wider
and taller. What a joy to those displaying merchandise to customers, or
handling the proliferating paperwork and record keeping, in a building
with an iron front *(fig. 1)*. Occasionally such a front was placed at both
ends of the building, as in the case of the still existing Cary Building,
105 Chambers Street in New York (Plate VII).

Cast iron was nonflammable and had great resistance to fire.
Properly cast, architectural elements weathered many fires, although
they were often dragged down by their burning surroundings. When
New York's block-square Wanamaker's store, with four facades of cast

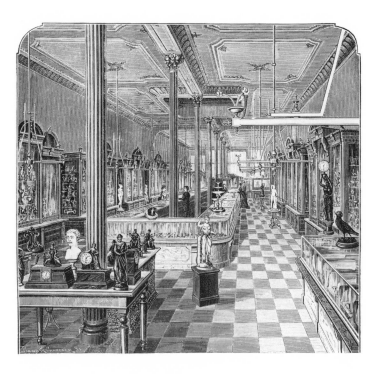

Fig. 1. Interior, Giles Bros. & Co.'s jewelry store, 266 & 268 Wabash Avenue, Chicago.

iron, caught fire during its demolition in 1956, the iron walls stood firm
for 24 hours as the conflagration raged out of control. Tons of water
were played onto the hot iron, enough to flood the subway below.
When the heat and smoke had cleared, the iron walls stood and had to
be knocked down by a wrecking ball. Inspection of photographs of the
ruins left by the Chicago Fire of 1871 discloses piles of stone and brick
with iron columns protruding from the rubble, apparently undamaged.
Recent research shows that people who owned iron-front buildings
before the Chicago Fire rebuilt with iron-front buildings after the fire,
seemingly satisfied with its performance under catastrophic conditions.

Cast-iron architectural construction had another virtue: it was
fast. The rapid expansion of commerce in this country in the latter half
of the nineteenth century had created a strong demand for business
structures for wholesalers' warehouses and for retail stores. Cast iron
could be prefabricated at the foundry and all its smaller elements pre-
assembled while the rest of the building—the brick sides and rear walls
and the floors and roof—was being constructed on the building site.
Then one fine day the iron would start coming in and as fast as it could
be delivered, the facade would be raised, bolted together and set in
place. The 1848 narrow five-story iron front on Dr. Milhau's pharmacy
on lower Broadway is reported to have been put up in three days. That
may have set some sort of record, but it does indicate the facility of the
construction process for iron fronts. It certainly cut down on labor costs
at the job, and was a far cry from the times when most of the items put
into a structure were handworked on the site. The Badger catalogue
enumerates these many advantages of iron architecture on pages 5
and 6.

Daniel D. Badger

Daniel Badger was a self-made man. A highly successful entre-
preneur, he emerges from what facts we have as a persistent and
aggressive businessman. Beginning as a blacksmith and a maker of
saws in Woburn, Mass., he built up a sizable business only to lose it in
a fire. Characteristically, he then made a big move, this time to Boston.
There he set up shop in 1830 on Cross Street at the corner of Fulton,
changing later to a larger place at 7 Haverhill Street, both locations being in industrial areas convenient to the water for receiving coal and
pig iron.

Badger advertised even then. In Boston city directories and
almanacs, he described himself as a blacksmith, handling everyday
work at the forge, and also as a whitesmith, producing ornamental
ironwork. It would be interesting to know which of Boston's lovely
wrought-iron fences and balconies done between 1830 and 1846 might

be attributable to him. After 1843 he added after his name in the city directory a listing as a manufacturer of patent rolling shutters. This agrees with the paragraph at the bottom of page 3 of his catalogue stating that A. L. Johnson of Baltimore showed Badger his patented rolling shutters, which the latter found to be just what he needed to fit into the iron storefronts he was already promoting. It seems that at once Badger bought Johnson's patent covering a product that was to become the Badger hallmark and which, together with the "Iron pillars and hollow posts," would soon be known in Boston as "Badger Fronts."

Ten or eleven years before he bought the shutters patent, Badger had devised his all-iron storefront. To add a bit of background: some 20 or 25 years earlier, Boston architect Alexander Parris had introduced the use of granite slabs for piers and lintels, constituting granite storefronts which opened the ground floor for larger windows than had been possible before. Greek Revival buildings all over the northeastern United States to this day reflect Parris' interesting new method, which found its greatest expression in his design for the Quincy Market (1824 –26) near Boston's waterfront. The markets recently have been spectacularly rehabilitated as shops and restaurants.

Parris' innovation was tremendous. In 1842 Daniel Badger made his own proposal utilizing the post-and-lintel system, but built with cast-iron members instead of granite. (This, it should be stressed, was a storefront rather than an entire facade.) It met with such skepticism that it is said on page 3 in the catalogue that Badger's first client agreed to this innovative iron construction only after Badger had guaranteed that he would remove it without cost if not satisfactory.

Iron storefronts had been used earlier in France for genteel small shops, and in England, where they were sometimes the choice for the

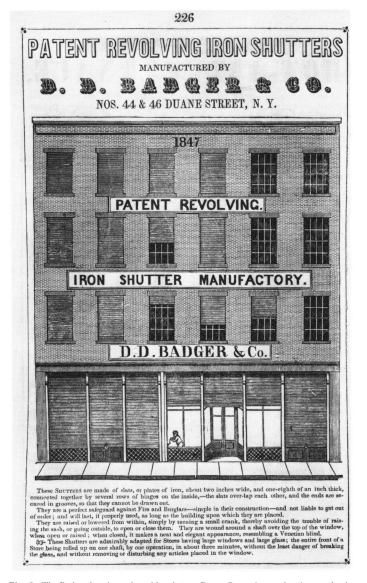

Fig. 2. *The Badger foundry and machine shop on Duane Street, in an advertisement for the rolling iron shutters.*

ground floor of a pub. In New York an advertisement for the sale of a building with an iron storefront appeared in an 1830 newspaper. The front of John Haviland's 1830 Mechanics Bank in Pottsville, Pa., was veneered with iron plates grooved and painted white to look like marble. In 1837, J. L. Mott placed his new iron storefront on display at the American Institute of N.Y. So if the catalogue's claim that Badger's storefront was the first iron construction in America seems too broad, perhaps one can assume that it was the first in his part of the country. As has happened in many fields of endeavor, minds were working along the same lines and coming to similar conclusions independently.

Badger's combination of his own iron storefront and Arthur L. Johnson's patent rolling shutters gave him a truly unique product, and I think that because he saw its potential he decided to take another giant step. In the mid-1840s he moved his business to New York. He is last listed in Boston city directories in 1848, and first listed in New York City directories in 1846, which makes one think that he tested the waters in New York before pulling out of Boston entirely.

Whether it colored his plans for moving, or whether the commission was evidence of his acumen as a salesman, the fact remains that one of Badger's earliest commissions was a door-opener for him. His Badger Fronts, tall fluted iron columns with grooves for his patent rolling shutters, constituted the ground-floor exterior of A. T. Stewart's imposing new marble department store in New York, which was attracting a great deal of attention as it was being built in 1845 to 1846 at the southeast corner of Reade Street and Broadway. It happened that Badger's little foundry and machine shop was but a short two blocks from the site at 42–46 Duane Street down a little hill from stylish Broadway where industry had crowded in (*fig. 2*). It also happened that Badger's rolling shutters had attracted favorable attention and a gold medal at the American Institute Fair of 1847.

The A. T. Stewart store, initially designed by Trench and Snook, is listed among Badger's jobs near the top of page 28. As Trench soon departed for the California Gold Rush, John Snook, a leading architect of the day, carried forward the work on the store and designed the decorative capitals of the iron columns in which the shutters were held. These are on Plate L, at the left of the page carrying the title The Stewart Capital, elsewhere (on page 14 the description of Plate L, No. 146) referred to as the Horn of Plenty Capital because of the cornucopias serving as volutes. The caduceus, an attribute of the god Mercury, is used as the symbol of commerce. Before the ceilings were lowered in the stores occupying the Stewart Building, now generally called The Sun Building, Horn of Plenty capitals could be seen atop the fluted columns on the interiors. Presumably they are still there, hidden by dropped acoustical-tile ceilings. They are also used on 14 exterior columns that can be clearly seen at nearby 100 Reade Street, a building that Snook erected for Stewart in 1859 also with ironwork by Badger. The contract with Badger called for $9,500; this is one of the few occasions on which we know his charges.

Badger built his first entire iron front in 1853, according to the chronicler of cast-iron construction, William J. Fryer, writing in 1898 in the *History of Real Estate, Building and Architecture in New York City* (p. 458). It was his first step beyond ground-floor storefronts with rolling shutters. Although that building is not identified, the six-story Gilsey Building (*fig. 3*), with two tall facades of iron at the southwest corner of Broadway and Cortlandt Street in Manhattan, in the heart of the business district, was erected around 1853. It does seem logical that a manufacturer would have undertaken a more modest project before attempting such a big New York office building. The Gilsey Building is seen on Plate IX, while details of the cornices at its first, third and top stories are depicted in drawings on Plate X, Nos. 84 and 85, and also on Plate XXXII, No. 50.

Unless business or family records not now known come to light, we will probably never know just when and in what order Badger's buildings were fabricated. It is perfectly clear, however, that when he branched out from making iron storefronts with rolling shutters into the making of total iron fronts he hit pay dirt. Fryer says, "No man connected with the business ever did as much as Mr. Badger to popularize the use of cast-iron fronts" (p. 458), and he goes on to add that "in his Architectural Iron Works men of talent were gathered as designers."

The *New York Times*, in its obituary of Badger, described him as a

Fig. 3. The Gilsey Building.

man of commanding presence and remarkable energy. This energy seems to have been addressed almost entirely to his business as he played no role in public affairs, devoting any spare time to his family and his church, the First Unitarian Church in Brooklyn Heights. The Badger family resided in Brooklyn from the time it moved from Boston to New York in 1848.

The 1850s were a period of prime importance in the iron industry as a whole, what with the proliferation of foundries, the increasing popularity of iron architecture, the final success in rolling iron beams and rails in America and the invention in England of the Bessemer process for making steel.

For Badger it was a time of almost incredible expansion, from the little four-story brick shop at 42 Duane Street into a large modern foundry that spread over the better part of a city block near the East River, between 13th and 14th Streets and Avenues B and C. The new foundry as it looked about 1854 is depicted in the opening pages of his catalogue. By this time he had already taken on George H. Johnson, the gifted young English architect from Manchester who designed so many of the individual modules reflected in the catalogue's illustrations of completed buildings. In 1856 Badger incorporated his business as the Architectural Iron Works of New York. In the same year he produced his most admired iron building, the Haughwout Store.

It is hard to determine what effect the Civil War had on Badger's foundry. Perhaps this impressive catalogue was issued in 1865 to give a lift to sagging business.

Lacking personal or corporation records, one can only surmise that business picked up, if indeed it ever slumped, for in the late 1860s we find the Architectural Iron Works executing some of its largest orders. These included the Gilsey Hotel on Broadway, the Powers office building in Rochester, the spectacular train shed of Grand Central Depot for Cornelius Vanderbilt and the ill-fated huge Manhattan Market at the edge of the Hudson River. All will be discussed later.

Apparently due to ill health that may have been aggravated by the financial panic of 1873 and possible problems brought on by intense competition from the many foundries that had grown up in the east, Badger retired from active business life in 1873.

Thereafter he seems to have lived quietly at his 191 Putnam Street home where, after a prolonged illness, pneumonia ended his life on November 19, 1884. His wife of 50 years survived him, as did two daughters and two sons.

The Architectural Iron Works in Action

Now let us turn back to the catalogue and begin by studying its wonderfully imaginative, evocative frontispiece, which gives an idea of the factory in action. It reveals a beehive of activity—the artist having concentrated on the galleries, the foundry floor and the basement beneath it, depicting the numerous processes that took place in various portions of the sprawling foundry of the Architectural Iron Works (shown in the following spread). He has, of course, used artistic license, for virtually all of this heavy activity, of necessity dictated by the weight and the size of the massive equipment, took place on the foundry floor. An engineer friend, Edward Hamilton, helped me interpret the activities depicted.

On the top balconies are typical post-and-lintel assemblies, probably representing shop-fitting of raw parts. One such is being raised to the right balcony on a gin pole and tackle, and a similar operation is seen on the middle balcony at the left, where a large lathe is in action and a drilling machine is being diligently cranked. They are being serviced by a stiff-leg crane. The pattern shop occupies the middle right balcony. At the back a patternmaker at his bench is engaged in hand work, which at that time accounted for the greatest amount of patternmaking. The big lathes are for wood turning, which comprised most of the balance of the work on patterns. The lathe in the foreground has elaborate gears propelled by a flat drive belt. In the background a workman raises a hammer; others wielding hammers can be seen scattered through the foundry. The artist seemed to like hammers, and also to like chimneys—eight of them are on the roof, smoking away.

Planning and consultation activities are prominently located in the forefront of the picture. Architects are discussing their working drawings with foundry representatives and clients are scattered among them, reacting to the designs. In this happiest of all foundries there are ladies in Victorian garb participating, looking over plans or strolling down the stairs, one with a parasol. Amidst all that hammering, grinding, assembling and transporting of iron pieces, it was a noisy place to carry on a conversation.

On the basement level, a foundry with two cupola furnaces is seen in the space on the left. A stiff-leg crane is maneuvering the ladle of molten metal and pouring it into a flask containing a sand mold. Another part of a mold, the "drag," lies open on the floor. The horse and cart appear to be taking out a load of sand. It has probably been used and reused many times and is now ready to be discarded. A workbench behind the horse and cart supports a large shear for cutting small bar stock or wire, basic to fence production.

In the right space on the basement level, wrought iron is being produced by the puddling process in three reverberatory furnaces. Two workmen strike blows to a wrought-iron part which a third man holds in position on the anvil. Although the Architectural Iron Works' stock in trade was cast-iron elements, wrought iron was produced for special structural uses, such as in bridges (Plates LXXXVI and LXXXVII) and in tension-rod girders, several versions of which are displayed in Plate LXIII. For these girders (sometimes called bowstring girders, for reasons No. 271 makes plain) a finished wrought-iron bar which would be serviceable in tension was laid into an open mold. When the mold had been closed, the compression member of cast iron would be poured around it.

The charming frontispiece employs Gothic forms, such as the pointed arches over the spiral stairs and the cast-iron tracery in the central archway, through which we glimpse Badger's office at 42 Duane Street after its face-lifting by architect John B. Snook in 1851. Taking Badger's small vernacular red brick structure, occupied when he first came to New York, Snook raised it one story and substituted an elaborate up-to-the-minute iron front of five stories employing a module created by Badger's in-house designer, George H. Johnson. Badger lists it in his catalogue on page 29, and Snook lists it in his account books, which can be seen at the New-York Historical Society. The module was later used on the elegant Cary Building.

Badger's Contemporaries

Had some of the other huge foundries produced such interesting and impressive visual records of their work as did Badger, they might now be equally well-known. For example, Hayward, Bartlett (later known as Bartlett, Robbins) created many large iron buildings, shipping them to various cities, including Portland, Ore., where their ornate Corbett Building stood for many years, and to Richmond, Va., where the post-Civil War ironfront Stearns Block was in 1976 converted into stylish air-conditioned offices. Another major Hayward, Bartlett iron front, the Robbins Building, is boarded up at the edge of Baltimore's Inner Harbor Urban Renewal Area, while the Fava Building, in the heart of the area, was recently disassembled for re-erection elsewhere. Yet librarians and scholars know of the existence of only one dog-eared copy of that founder's tiny pocket catalogue. And few outside Baltimore have ever heard of Hayward, Bartlett.

As another instance, the Cornell Ironworks, which filled two square city blocks on the west side of Manhattan on the Hudson River at 26th Street and also acquired the West Point Foundry in Cold Spring, N.Y., left no catalogues that have come to light thus far. We know several jobs they handled, including the block square 1862 A. T. Stewart iron store on Broadway at East 10th Street, and occasionally we run across contemporary references to their work or find their labels embossed at the base of a column or doorway. But the Cornell brothers are virtually forgotten, while Badger is remembered.

Because we can see so clearly in his catalogue many of the impressive examples of Badger's completed iron architecture, it behooves us to remind ourselves that others were doing big things, too, and weigh his accomplishments with those of others less well advertised such as the Cornells or his early neighbor Adrian Janes, whose foundry, by then known as Janes, Kirtland and located in the Bronx, would produce the powerful iron dome of the United States Capitol as well as the entirely iron Congressional Library constructed within the Capitol in 1852.

The Catalogue

Badger had several reasons for publishing this handsome and expensive catalogue of a caliber far exceeding what anyone else in the business had published in this country. In the last paragraph of the introduction (page 9) it is stated that the purpose of the catalogue was twofold: it was issued as a means for supplying architects with details for the construction of iron buildings, and also served as a merchandising medium for the foundry. Besides wanting to build up his business with this extravagant piece of advertising, Badger may also have hoped to establish his place in the history of cast-iron architecture, something which we can agree he has accomplished.

The *Illustrations of Iron Architecture* came out in 1865. That Badger and his firm had attracted a great deal of business up to the time the catalogue was issued is attested by the many large iron structures that he was able to present in it as completed work. There has been speculation as to whether most of the buildings pictured in the book were new designs waiting to be ordered or whether they had actually been constructed before being depicted. The latter was the case, and by now most of them have been accounted for. Some still exist, others are known to have existed although they are now gone, while only a few designs seem never to have been built.

The importance of this catalogue derives from several aspects. Foremost, of course, are the illustrations—large-scale, clear, well-drawn and very informative. They were reproduced as lithographs by the leading firm of Sarony, Major & Knapp of 449 Broadway in New York City, which at the time ranked with Currier & Ives in the field.

In its 102 pages of plates are presented 38 buildings having total iron facades. Along with these are 51 designs for ground-floor iron storefronts, and in the listings of principal works Badger records the 654 storefronts built by the firm by 1865. The cast-iron storefront was of course less expensive and less spectacular than the complete facades, and was far more widely used by architects and builders all over the United States. Storefronts must have constituted a large proportion of the work of this or any foundry.

The nature of the individual iron sections of buildings is shown on page after page of detailed drawings of cornices, balustrades, window arches and keystones, spandrels, consoles and brackets, columns and capitals, window lintels and sills, together with such accessories as lamps, urns, even sidewalks. Any one of these sections would of necessity be an assembly of many smaller individual castings, the number sometimes running into scores of castings if the section were a large one, such as a length of elaborate cornice (for example, Plate X, No. 97, which shows a corner of the cornice on the Haughwout Building, 490 Broadway, shown in its entirety in Plate III) or the module of the Cary Building (Plate VIII, No. 118, the entire building shown in Plate VII).

If there is one plate in the book that should evoke admiration above all, it is perhaps not that of the imposing iron fronts themselves, or that of the ornate Venetian window tracery in iron, nor that of the cast-iron bridges, but Plate LI, which shows the grand 10-, 12- and even 14-foot-tall iron columns offered by the Architectural Iron Works. These are masterpieces of both the patternmaker's and the iron caster's art and at the same time were the workhorses of the whole system of cast-iron architecture.

Cast iron can bear up under tremendous loads. It has been calculated that a column of iron would have to be a mile high before the metal at its base was crushed. As cast-iron architecture is essentially a post-and-lintel system, it is those posts, those columns, that are the kingpins, be they as fragile-looking as those for the Billing & Co. storefront (Plate LXXIV) or as massive as the 14-foot-tall fluted Corinthian-type on pedestals at the former Haughwout Building. These columns are masterpieces because of the great skill required to produce them. They were cast in hard-to-handle flasks (the foundryman's term for the wooden case holding the sand mold) that were longer than the column was tall. The columns had to be true as a die, and inasmuch as they were hollow (this aspect of their manufacture called for the tricky business of using cores in casting), their side walls had to be of uniform thickness so that they would not bend or collapse under great loads. Over and above all this, these columns had to be beautiful, perhaps fluted, with ornate capitals.

The illustrations in this catalogue are its paramount aspect and teach us a great deal about the subject of cast-iron architecture. But because there is virtually no caption information on the individual plates, the serious reader is urged to refer back and forth between the illustrations and the printed material at the front of the catalogue, for in this way much information can be pieced together. In addition, he can correlate some of the illustrations in this catalogue with photographs and text concerning several of Badger's existing buildings that are included in *Cast-Iron Architecture in New York* (Dover 22980-7).

The importance of this catalogue also lies in the 12-page listing, beginning on page 23, of cast-iron architecture completed by the Architectural Iron Works up to 1865. It lets us know that cast-iron architecture was extremely popular and that the Architectural Iron Works was one of the country's most prolific producers of cast-iron architecture. It also lets us know something about where iron structures were in demand. The completed buildings are listed under the cities where they were erected, and the cities themselves are listed alphabetically. They range from Albany, N.Y. (listing a four-story iron front on Pearl St. that stands) and Alexandria, La. (where a courthouse portico of iron was provided) to Washington, D.C. (where ironwork was erected in Ford's Theatre not long before President Lincoln was assassinated there) and Wilmington, N.C. (a Mr. Barry's little iron storefront). In between, 650 examples are listed for 67 localities, including Canada, Cuba, Brazil, Panama and Egypt.

A quick glance through the list discloses that nine out of ten of the jobs included are one-story iron storefronts. The entire top-to-bottom iron facade was not as frequent as some writers would have us believe when they claim that iron-front buildings lined the streets of old downtown districts toward the end of the nineteenth century.

From perusing this valuable list we also observe that the Architectural Iron Works had other capabilities, such as bridge building and the erection of grain elevators, ferry houses, arsenals and markets. Although these capabilities were not often utilized, such large public works did show to advantage when the foundry was given the opportunity to produce them, as in the case of the big grain warehouses in

Brooklyn and Philadelphia (Plates LX, LXI, LXII) and the arsenal storehouse still to be seen at Watervliet (Plate XII).

This catalogue provides valuable information on practicing architects of the 1850s and 1860s in various parts of the country, most particularly in New York City, where the preponderance of the Architectural Iron Works' jobs were located. Many of the structures in the list of completed work are coupled with their architects. It becomes apparent which architects favored this innovative material—again and again we see the names of John B. Snook, Samuel A. Warner, John Kellum, Gamaliel King, Robert G. Hatfield, F. A. Petersen, John Van Osdel, George H. Johnson, G. J. F. Bryant, Charles Mettam, J. F. Duckworth and others. Too little is known about these practitioners, so that this catalogue, especially through its illustrations, sheds considerable light on their work. In that day, architects received little credit for their efforts, and it has been suggested that Daniel Badger and the Architectural Iron Works were very astute in publicly listing these men who were their customers, and may have made loyal friends of them.

Under the aegis of its founder and president Daniel D. Badger, the firm did attract an enormous volume of work both before and after the catalogue was issued. Abner Ely, the original head of the famous New York real-estate management firm that is still headed by a member of the Ely family, reported to his client Charles Moulton on February 21, 1854, that he would try to get Daniel Badger's foundry to do the ornamental ironwork for the ground floor of the new building at 550 Broadway which Moulton expected to lease to Tiffany's store, but that "he has so much business that it is difficult to get the work done." Nonetheless, Badger did get it done, as can be seen on Plate LXIV, No. 26.

After the publication of this, the only catalogue that Badger is known to have issued, the firm received commissions for some of the largest iron buildings in this country, so its publication must have generated strong interest and confidence both in iron as a building material and in the Architectural Iron Works as one of its leading fabricators. Four post-publication commissions, which will be discussed later, were the eight-story iron-front Gilsey Hotel, the great arching train shed of the first Grand Central Railroad Depot, and the block-long, wide-span Manhattan Produce Market, all in New York City, as well as the Powers Building in Rochester, N.Y.

Before we turn to an examination of various important Badger buildings, we might describe the original volume from which this reprint is made. It was a large-format hardcover volume of 33 pages of text followed by 102 pages of plates printed on one side only by the lithographic process. A simulation of a monochromatic watercolor wash was given to those plates that depicted large iron-front structures, and multicoloration was given to the frontispiece.

Surely the size of the catalogue and the fact that it was bound in hard covers, together with its outstanding lithographs, contributed to the survival of several copies when other more prosaically produced paperbound foundry catalogues were discarded once their immediate usefulness was past. Often these were little more than pamphlets, such as those produced by the Eagle Iron Works of Buffalo or the Chase Brothers Co. of Boston. Others were put out in the form of pocket catalogues for the convenience of salesmen and architects, as in the case of Bartlett, Robbins in Baltimore or Bouton's Union Iron Works in Chicago. On the other hand, J. L. Mott did issue some hardcover catalogues of his decorative fountains and urns, and J. B. Wickersham published in hard cover an 80-page catalogue entitled *A New Phase in the Iron Manufacture.*

Copies of *Illustrations of Iron Architecture* are rare. There is to my knowledge a copy of the original at the New York Public Library, another at the Boston Public Library, a third at the Avery Architectural Library at Columbia University, a fourth at the Library of Congress (undoubtedly deposited there for copyright purposes in 1865) and another at the Fine Arts Library of Cornell University. It would be helpful to learn of other copies that may exist.

Iron-Front Buildings by the Architectural Iron Works

Which of the buildings pictured in the catalogue still exist? Sadly, not too many, yet more than might be expected, given the nature of our throwaway society and the disdain with which Victorian architecture was regarded until ten or fifteen years ago.

Without question the finest of the existing iron-front commercial buildings produced by the Architectural Iron Works (or any other foundry for that matter) is the Haughwout Building *(fig. 4)* at 490 Broadway and the northeast corner of Broome Street in Manhattan (Plate III). Its corner location allows it to have two ornate iron walls, embracing five stories of diminishing height, comprised of a single module repeated 92 times across the two facades. It is very elegant. Keystone arches spring from small, slender fluted Corinthian columns and are set between tall Corinthian columns on paneled pedestals joined visually by a balustrade course at each story. The module is reminiscent of Sansovino's library on the Piazzetta in Venice, and the building itself has the aspect of a Venetian palazzo rising beside the Grand Canal.

Fig. 4. *The Haughwout Building.*

It was built in 1856 by Walter Langdon, Jr., who had inherited the land from his grandfather, John Jacob Astor. 490 Broadway has been owned by only two families: Astor descendents and members of the Cahn family, which purchased it in 1943. Langdon entrusted the development of this key piece of real estate, then in the heart of the retail and hotel district, to Abner Ely, the famous real-estate manager who ordered the iron fronts from Daniel Badger. With architect John P. Gaynor, who would soon move west and create the spectacular Palace Hotel in San Francisco, he provided a large retail emporium with a sweeping interior double stairway leading to upper floors through a central light well, tailored to the needs of its first tenant, Eder V. Haughwout. With Francis Nichol and William Davidson, Haughwout conducted a luxurious store selling silver, china, mirrors, bronzes, chandeliers and objets d'art. Haughwout did not deal in jewelry—that was the province of Louis Tiffany, whose store was a block to the north. The Haughwout Store furnished many fine homes and hotels, and when in May 1861 Mrs. Lincoln shopped for a new china pattern for the White House, she came to Haughwout's and ordered a spread-eagle design bordered in her favorite shade of mauve. Haughwout had exhibited it at the Crystal Palace in 1853.

No significant change has been made to the exterior of the Haughwout building. Recently the Cahn family had it repainted, a horrendously expensive job because of the sculptured nature of the building's facades. They chose black. Before the new coat was put on, the peeling paint disclosed white paint of an even earlier vintage. However, we know that the original color was the now-forgotten Victorian favorite called "drab." To make this color, A. J. Downing wrote, to white paint "add burnt umber, Indian red and a little black."

In this century the Haughwout Building has housed light industry and now contains a fabric business. It was designated a landmark in November 1965 as the Landmarks Preservation Commission sought to protect it from the imminent threat of the proposed Cross-Manhattan Expressway, which after that never materialized. It was recorded by The Historic American Building Survey in 1968, and is on the National Register of Historic Places.

The Cary Building, shown on Plate VII, can be seen at 105 Chambers Street at the northwest corner of Church Street in Manhattan, not far from City Hall. It is unusual in that it presents identical back and front iron facades on Chambers Street and on Reade Street. Except for harsh changes in the ground floor, the two exterior iron walls still look like their picture in the catalogue. Clearly they were designed to resemble masonry, horizontal areas above each tier of windows being scored to simulate blocks of laid-up ashlar. The knowing eye is not fooled: the frail fluted columns from which the arches spring would be so hard to produce in stone, so easy to make in iron. The graceful, tall fluted columns on the ground floor also would be too frail in stone — these columns are supporting the four-story facade above. As I was able to observe when this building was being given a rather heavy-handed face-lift recently, each column is attached to a weblike iron support at right angles behind it. These strengthen the columns and until that time helped contain the mechanism for the famed Badger rolling shutters which still had all mechanical elements intact. In the plate, the patent shutters are shown at many openings, some closed entirely, some partway.

Both the Cary and the Haughwout Buildings were built in 1856 and are the oldest iron fronts standing in Manhattan now that the 1849 Bogardus-Laing Stores have been lost through an egregious bureaucratic error. Judging from their placement at the front of the catalogue, Badger was very proud of them. Gamaliel King, a leading Brooklyn architect, teamed with a younger partner, John Kellum, to produce the Cary Building, which employs iron fashioned in a design unit (Plate VIII, No. 118) thought to be from the pencil of George H. Johnson, staff architect with Badger. That same design module is to be seen on the tall, skinny iron front at 620 Broadway, just north of Houston

Street. Architect John B. Snook utilized it when erecting this building for Henry Dolan in 1857. It is listed on page 27. Snook used it earlier for Badger's own premises at 42 Duane Street.

An exceptionally well-proportioned iron front of five stories designed for the standard 25-foot New York building lot is depicted in Plate XV, No. 8. It was built at 93 Reade Street, Manhattan, for a man named John Q. Jones in 1857, which means that it was going up as the Cary Building was being finished next door. They stand side by side and complement each other to an unusual degree. The leaves of the fluted columns have been stripped from their bells.

Not far away, at 120 Chambers Street, is the building illustrated on Plate XC, somewhat the worse for wear. The ground floor is bastardized. Because, like the Cary Building, this structure runs right through the block and has matching iron fronts on two streets, it is worth taking a walk to the back on Warren Street, where less change has been made. Various decorations seem to be missing and leaves have been removed from the bells of the fluted pilasters.

Up the Hudson River in Watervliet, a suburb of Troy, N.Y., is an old U.S. Army installation called Watervliet Arsenal. Here one can enjoy the experience of seeing an all-iron building, the ideal of many nineteenth-century inventors and iron founders (fig. 5). It is the Watervliet Storage House (Plates XII and XIII), which came about through the chance meeting at West Point of the Arsenal's new commanding officer and J. M. Reed, president of the Architectural Iron Works, in October 1857, a year when the foundry could boast many achievements. It might be noted here that Badger often used the title Superintendent.

The commanding officer was Major Alfred Mordecai, who wanted a totally fireproof warehouse for storage of new gun carriages awaiting shipment. He drew plans for a storage house that would be durable, fireproof and ornamental and "sold" his superiors on an unorthodox structure (Plate XXIX), made with iron plates and paired pilasters for walls, and many iron-enframed floor-to-ceiling windows for natural illumination, with rolling iron shutters for security. The building also featured iron stairs and sheet-iron gable sheathing and sheet-iron roof, carried on wrought-iron trusses supported by cast-iron pillars. He also got the price reduced from an estimate of $60,000 to the $47,360 which was actually paid. We are fortunate in having specific information about this building from federal records: the exact amount paid for the iron parts, their shipment and final assembly on the foundation provided. We know also that the contract was signed in January 1859 and the job completed before August, which is to say in eight months, for in January work on cutting patterns for molding had begun at the foundry on East 14th Street in New York City. Casting of the iron parts continued into the spring when smaller parts were readied and assembled. As spring thaws opened the Hudson for traffic, shipments of completed iron sections started upriver for Watervliet. The 100-by-196-foot rectangular storage house, well adapted for its

Fig. 5. The Watervliet Storage House.

Fig. 6. Interior, the Watervliet Storage House.

purpose, rose on the foundations provided by the Army and has been in service ever since. The interior *(fig. 6)* is well worth studying. Beside the truss system of the roof, there are cast-iron girders with wrought-iron tension rods similar to those illustrated on Plate LXIII, No. 273. The Arsenal has been recorded by the Historic American Engineering Record and is documented in *The Mohawk-Hudson Area Survey*, edited by Robert M. Vogel of the Smithsonian. It is open to the public by appointment.

A fire in the summer of 1862 in Bath, a pretty town in New York's Finger Lakes section, swept away an entire business block. As in so many cases of nineteenth-century fires, iron architecture provided good-looking replacement buildings quickly and at a moderate cost. Architect George Bartlett rebuilt A. W. Howell's store at 7 Liberty Street, selecting a Venetian-style module from the array offered by D. D. Badger's foundry. The ornate iron front was delivered in 62 pieces, its erection early in 1863 attracting much interest in the local press. As can be seen on Plate XVII, No. 6, it is embellished with lion heads, wreathes, vines and bunches of grapes. D'Angelo's restaurant now occupies it, printing its history in its menu, and keeps it painted a proper Victorian drab color with decorative details picked out in naturalistic colors. Architects Roger Reed and Michael Herschensohn have described it in their survey of significant architecture in Bath.

Albany, N.Y. has only one surviving iron-front building although at one time it had several. This iron front, now undergoing refurbishing, was built for James Kidd at 51 North Pearl Street in 1861, when the characteristic Dutch-style and Federal houses on the street were replaced by prestigious commercial properties *(fig. 7)*. Badger supplied the 45-foot-wide iron front to be fitted onto a brick structure (Plate XXI). An additional floor which has a portrait bust of George Washington in its pediment has been added.

The experienced New York architect John Kellum, who favored cast-iron architecture, designed a dramatic building for Condict Brothers' large saddlery at 55 White Street in Manhattan, pictured in Plate CII. Built in 1861 in a characteristic Kellum style, it has giant smooth columns rising through two stories, one tier on top of another, set on a trabeated ground floor, now, alas, covered by modern materials. Faceted quoins mark the edges of the building, which has Romanesque corbeling beneath the strong cornice. Badger may have regarded it as an appropriate climax for his catalogue, placing it as he did at the very end.

A last survivor in New York City is 77 Chambers Street, which has weathered much abuse and scarcely is recognizable as Plate XXXVIII, No. 9.

A happier note can be struck concerning a small building in Halifax, Nova Scotia, built to the design of Plate LXXIX. It is a charming front with a bold half-circle fan window lighting the entire second story. All is delicacy and daintiness, from the slender pillars of the ground floor to the rinceau in the frieze beneath the cornice and the faintly Greek Revival acroteria above it. It stands in a row of commercial buildings put up following a destructive 1859 fire on Granville Street. Restoration of the street is contemplated. After that fire Badger

Fig. 7. 51 North Pearl Street, Albany.

fronts must have gotten a big boost as being nonflammable, ornate and fast to set in place, for 12 of them are listed under Halifax on pages 24 and 25 of the catalogue. Alas, all have now been altered beyond recognition.

A calamitous fire also spurred the use of cast iron in Richmond. After the Civil War the city turned to iron fronts as a means of rebuilding with alacrity following its evacuation. Retiring Confederate troops had burned Richmond's business areas as Union forces entered the city. The lovely iron front in Plate LXXIX, the same as in Halifax, was the first put up on ruined Main Street when Richmond's rebuilding began in 1866. It can be glimpsed only in old photographs, for it is gone now. Six other iron fronts on Main Street survived. They are in the style of iron buildings erected in Chicago eight or nine years before and are depicted in the catalogue. Of these, three constitute Richmond's spectacularly restored Stearns Block at 1007–1013 East Main Street, now an air-conditioned, fully tenanted modern office building, which employs the same design module as that seen on Plate LIV. Pretty 1015 East Main Street also uses it. There is a mystery here, for although this building is shown in Badger's catalogue, building contracts document it as produced by the Hayward, Bartlett foundry of Baltimore. A possible resolution of the mystery rests with George H. Johnson, Badger's English-born designer, who was also the proven architect of the Richmond buildings. Did he in some way control the patterns made to his designs or borrow or lease them from Badger? We have much to learn about relationships in the architectural iron business, and few papers or financial records to rely on. It is fortunate that a handful of the sales catalogues such as this have survived.

Some of the structures included in the list beginning on page 23 of the catalogue were not illustrated, but still exist and can be seen by the devotee of cast-iron architecture. In 1860 a large resort hotel had been built near the popular mineral springs in Sharon, N.Y. for H. J. Bangs of New York City. Three years later he had a cast-iron pavilion designed by architect Lawrence Burgher and shipped in pieces from the Architectural Iron Works for assembly in the hotel's lovely grounds, to shade Magnesia Springs (fig. 8). There it remains, its tall Italianate arches invaded by the lush trees and flowering shrubs that were planted around it so many years ago. Above its low pediment rises an octagonal drum surmounted by a dome which has a balustraded lookout and a finial at its very top. The hotel burned in 1873. The pavilion has survived, but for how much longer?

The famous Cooper Union, built between 1853 and 1859, is an Italianate brownstone structure in lower Manhattan. The facade on the ground floor is a 326-foot arcade of cast-iron arches that spring from pilasters with Composite capitals. Peter Cooper envisioned them as defining a series of small stores that would bring in revenue needed to maintain his free school, which occupied the upper floors. It never quite worked out that way and now the school's library fills most of the ground floor. Great sheets of modern plate glass have been put into the openings. This commission from the respected, almost adulated, Peter Cooper, along with that from A. T. Stewart, must have helped Badger in his early days. It is listed on page 32 of the catalogue, where he records that he did "all Inside Cast Iron Work" as well as the exterior arcade.

Two other big iron-front buildings that I have visited and therefore know to exist are listed in the catalogue but without illustration. Both are receiving more attention now than in many decades; both are on the National Register of Historic Places.

One is in Mobile, Ala. at 51 Dauphin Street. Built in 1860 for Daniels, Elgin Drygoods Store, it is listed on page 25. Its architect, J. H. Giles, later designed the ornate old Lord & Taylor Store, still to be seen on Broadway in New York City. Present owners of the Mobile edifice have modernized it as an office building. The iron parts for this Italianate front were probably shipped by water from the foundry to this Gulf Coast city.

Milwaukee's Ironblock is identified in the list as similar to Plate XLVI. Built in 1860–61 at 205 East Wisconsin Avenue at the corner of Water Street, it has five floors of iron with rows of very tall arched windows. It has been named a Landmark by the Milwaukee Landmarks Commission. In the case of this and virtually all of the existing buildings mentioned, the Friends of Cast Iron Architecture has played a role in identifying their historical and architectural significance and in supporting efforts to preserve them.

The embossed Badger name or that of the Architectural Iron Works is to be observed on iron storefronts on old streets in downtown Manhattan too frequently to list the addresses here, although 99 Reade Street and 38 Walker Street might be mentioned. Sometimes in a distant city the Badger label will catch your eye. For instance, very difficult to discern, but definitely there, is the Badger label on the base of an iron pier of a romantically arranged old store that has come to be Norman Belli's law office in San Francisco. It is adjacent to the Jackson

Fig. 8. Pavilion, Magnesia Springs.

Square area, which escaped the post-Earthquake fire in 1906. On little Strawberry Street, just off Chestnut Street in Philadelphia, the Badger label is quite clear on an interesting old L-shaped building (built for W. W. Keen, according to the note on page 34). In Savannah, 121 Congress Street has an iron storefront signed by Badger and a similar mark is to be found on the iron store fronts on Middle Street in Portland, Me.

There are several major iron-front buildings by the Architectural Iron Works built after the catalogue's 1865 publication that I would like to mention because they still exist.

Noteworthy among these is the old Gilsey House, a flamboyant iron-and-marble eight-story hotel built by Peter Gilsey, the Danish-American merchant who gave Badger one of his earliest big commissions for a total iron front, the 1853 Gilsey Building on lower Broadway. Gilsey's Hotel was built in 1869 on the uptown edge of the theater district, on Broadway at 29th Street. Across its sculptured facade architect Stephen Hatch deployed coupled columns, Palladian windows, broken pediments and urns, a clock and a slate mansard roof of noble proportions (fig. 9). It attracted not only theatrical people but "army and navy officers, congressmen and railroad magnates." After 1911 it housed a conglomeration of small factories, but now some enterprising young developers have converted it into a luxury loft co-op.

Fig. 10. 90 Maiden Lane.

Fig. 9. The Gilsey House.

No. 319 Broadway is an iron-front building at the northwest corner of Thomas Street, near New York's City Hall. It too went up in 1869, one of identical twins on opposite corners of this little street that had for decades been the carriageway into the landscaped grounds of the New York Hospital, the city's first such institution. When the hospital moved uptown the grounds were cut up and immediately built upon, the two office buildings being the work of architect brothers David and John Jardine. The northern twin looks sad for lack of maintenance, but the fate of its southern twin was sadder, for it was demolished in 1974 to make room for a fast-food restaurant.

One other known Badger iron front is in the financial district at 90 Maiden Lane (fig. 10). A perennially good-looking little gem designed in 1872 for James Alfred Roosevelt, it was a classic example of modernization of an older structure by fitting it with a new iron front, in this case the two old brick buildings where Cornelius V. S. Roosevelt had opened a glassware and mirror store in 1815. The graceful symmetrical design by Charles Wright employs very slender iron elements, so that the facade is virtually all glass. It benefits greatly from the good maintenance provided by its owner, the Continental Insurance Company.

In Rochester, N.Y., Daniel Powers built an iron-front commercial building to which he continued to add for years, both laterally and vertically, always determined to have the tallest building in town. Badger provided the iron for both fronts on State and Main Streets, and also for the sweeping, monumental interior iron staircase that spirals from the ground floor to the top story, where Powers enjoyed displaying his significant art collection. Rochester architect Andrew Jackson Warner designed the Powers Building in 1869 and it has formed a cornerstone of downtown Rochester ever since. It is on the National Register of Historic Places.

Finally, I can mention two other existing Badger iron-front buildings. Perhaps readers can add others. One is in Boston. The Boston Post Building, a unique little iron front at 17 Milk Street opposite Old South Meeting House, perhaps no more than 18 feet wide, was built very rapidly right after the great Boston Fire of October 1872. The Architectural Iron Works supplied the front and was proud of its ornate decoration, including a bust of Franklin that still adorns the second story, an appropriate ornament for a newspaper's headquarters, especially this one on the site of his birthplace.

The other is in Chicago: the drastically altered iron-front Page Brothers Leather Store with a 70-foot frontage on Lake Street, at the southeast corner of State Street. Built on the burned-out site of the famed old City Hotel after the Great Fire of 1871, it faced the impressive row of Frederick Tuttle's post-Fire iron fronts (fig. 11) and was part of Chicago's reaffirmation of its satisfaction with iron as a building material. Of the city's numerous post-Fire iron fronts, Page's is the only one left. Preservationists have only recently identified it and tried to draw attention to Chicago's lone remaining iron front before redevelopment destroys it. The Chicago architect John Van Osdel, who once worked in New York, had built in iron in 1856 and 1857, placing a monumental order with Badger for one five-story iron front building after another to meet Chicago's mounting demand for commercial space at mid-century. They were all wiped out in the Great Fire, but plates depicting four of them appear in the catalogue and give us an idea of the grandeur of these structures compared with the small brick and wooden buildings around them when they first went up (Plates LIV, VII, XIX and LXX, all listed under Chicago on page 24. Although the pediment in Plate VII bears the name Cary, the building is identical to that built in Chicago. The module used was Badger's most popular.)

Fig. 11. Cast-iron fronts, East Lake Street, Chicago, 1870s.

Fig. 12. A train passes the Halsey Building, Brooklyn.

There is a final category: significant buildings that are recorded in the catalogue but have been demolished. I will describe those that I have investigated by means of documents and old pictures which prove that they were, in fact, built. These include the dramatic assembly of Chicago iron buildings just mentioned. In addition, there was the five-story Fireman's Insurance Building at 211 Camp Street in New Orleans. Venetian in inspiration with plate tracery in its windows, the arches of which sprang from dainty coupled columns, we know that it was built by Paul Tulane before 1865, as it appears on page 25, and that it was demolished in 1900. There was also the early Halsey Building (fig. 12) on Fulton Street in Brooklyn, a splendid iron facade overlooking Brooklyn City Hall (now known as Borough Hall) and its park. The prominent Halsey family built this long five-story front in 1856 as an office building. It became popular with lawyers because it was so convenient to City Hall and the courts. Architect John P. Gaynor's advertisements of 1857 spoke of the Halsey Building and the Haughwout Building as special accomplishments. Both, it will be noted by comparing Plates LII and III, have iron fronts composed of exactly the same Palladian-style module. George H. Johnson is named as an architect in the listing on page 24, which makes me think that as Badger's designer he created the module and that Gaynor employed it to advantage in two quite different buildings which he designed in 1856. I would say he had a good eye, and chose the cream of the crop. The Halsey Building was demolished after World War II, when the Brooklyn Civic Center was expanded and totally redesigned.

Another victim of this redevelopment around Brooklyn Borough Hall was the Kings County Court House on Joralemon Street, a stone's throw from the Halsey Building. Gamaliel King and Herman J. Tecknitz, Brooklyn architects, won a competition for its design in 1861 and utilized iron framing for its roof and dome. The combination of cast-iron columns for the interior and the wrought-iron trusses for the roof and elements of the dome were supplied by the Architectural Iron Works. It was sad to see it being demolished in 1961 and reflect that this sturdy marble classical revival building, built for the ages, had lasted merely 100 years. The Brooklyn Law School occupies its site.

The Gilsey Building of the early 1850s (Plate IX) was demolished in 1907 during construction of the City Investing Company Building, which in turn gave way to the present 54-story U.S. Steel's black skyscraper at Broadway and Cortlandt Street. In 1892, the charming little Grover & Baker Sewing Machine Co. iron building, built in 1860 to designs by George H. Johnson at 495 Broadway, came down. This confection of Gothic metal tracery and expanses of imported plate-glass windows, where ladies were escorted by their husbands to observe and even take lessons on sewing machines, is pictured on Plate XI.

Manhattan had innumerable ferry lines connecting it with the City of Brooklyn, with Staten Island and with New Jersey on the mainland until today's great bridges and tunnels were built. There was often confusion with multiplicity of ownership and less-than-efficient service. The Union Ferry Company was formed by leading citizens to handle the situation and in 1863 and 1864 it ordered two new ferry terminals built. John Kellum was commissioned to design them and the Architectural Iron Works got the job of executing his designs for these virtually all-iron structures.

The Fulton Ferry, which traversed the East River from Fulton Street in Manhattan to Fulton Street in Brooklyn, was given a long, low Italianate iron building painted tan with brown trim (fig. 13). It

Fig. 13. The Fulton Ferry terminal.

had a central pavilion marked by a low pediment. This was flanked by entrances to two ferry slips and had a pleasing circular canopy over its main entrance. End pavilions also had low pediments and bull's-eye windows. The structure is listed in the catalogue on page 30.

We know so little about the costs of iron architecture in its day that it is of extreme interest to learn from a book, *The Historical Sketch of the Fulton Ferry*, that this building cost $39,000, much of which must have gone to the Architectural Iron Works.

South Ferry, the point from which ferries crossed the harbor to Staten Island and to distant Fort Hamilton in Brooklyn, was a significant location. The Union Ferry Company spent $73,000 for a flamboyant four-towered iron building embracing a pair of ferry slips for each destination. The whole facade is so fancy and so prettied-up that it looks like an exhibition building at a fair. Arches and paneling and canopied entrances, fan windows and perforated towers with domes from which fly pennants—all can be seen in old prints and stereographic views. It is listed in the catalogue on page 33. The Architectural Iron Works took pride in this large municipal contract and I am surprised that at least one of these resplendent ferry houses did not get a plate in the catalogue. Perhaps their completion came too late.

As Cornelius Vanderbilt undertook to put together a railroad empire, he purchased four lines feeding into New York City. A central terminal became his goal. The tracks were relaid so that all could come onto the island over a new swing bridge which he built across the Harlem River, then to 97th Street by way of a stone viaduct and on to 42nd Street through an open cut along what is now Park Avenue. In 1869 his Grand Central Depot began to rise at 42nd Street. The station itself, of brick and stone, was large, not very efficient, and more than a little pompous in appearance. John B. Snook designed it. The train shed was something else: designed probably by Isaac C. Buckout and fabricated in the Architectural Iron Works. It was an engineering masterpiece and unprecedented on this continent.

It was derived directly from the soaring train shed of St. Pancras Station in London, which to this day thrills the visitor who sees it for the first time. The Badger train shed at Grand Central built about five years later was not much smaller, being 200 feet in width, the same 100 feet in height and 600 feet long. There is no doubt that it aroused the interest of Americans, for Carroll Meeks reports in his book *The Railroad Station* that it was the largest interior space on this continent and a tourist attraction second only to the Capitol in Washington. It was pictured in wood engravings in all the illustrated periodicals. The light covering of sheet iron and glass arching over 12 tracks and five platforms was carried on 30 Howe trusses of wrought iron *(fig. 14)*. Their ends were tied together by wrought-iron tie rods that ran under the tracks through pipes that protected them from moisture and from being shaken by passing trains.

The rear, or uptown, end of the train shed, at about 45th Street, was closed off by a curtain wall of ornate cast iron and sheet metal that protected travelers on the platforms from wind and weather *(fig. 15)*. It had pediments and urns and a large fanlight window in the central gable beneath the legend "Erected 1871." This station was replaced by the present Grand Central Terminal, which opened in 1913.

Although the train shed was built five years after the catalogue was published, it does figure prominently in Badger's obituaries. That in the *American Architect and Building News* states that the contract price for the ironwork was worth more than a million dollars, while the *New York Times* obituary adds that Badger had 1500 men employed on the Grand Central Depot job.

The last big structure that I identify with Badger and his Architectural Iron Works is Manhattan Market *(fig. 16)*. This is a building that is gone and also forgotten, having stood only eight years. Structurally it had much in common with Grand Central's train shed, for it had a 90-foot-tall trussed wrought-iron semicircular vault, perfect for an indoor market space. Exterior dimensions of the brick-and-iron walls

Fig. 14. Interior, train shed, Grand Central Terminal.

Fig. 15. Uptown end, train shed, Grand Central Terminal.

were, according to the *New York Times*, 200 by 800 feet. With aisles on both sides under pitched roofs and some 50 feet at each end devoted to administrative purposes, the spectacular wide-span vault seems to have been about 180 feet in width and 600 feet long.

The market's main entrance was on Eleventh Avenue between 34th and 35th Streets and the back faced its pier on the Hudson River. Its exterior was most picturesque, with arcades along all streets, a design readily executed in iron. A square tower marked each corner and rose high with a peaked roof. At each side-street entrance there was an arched cornice topped by a spirelet, and rising in the very center was a tall dome, made even taller by its lantern and finial. The roof featured long monitor systems for light and ventilation.

Manhattan market opened in November of 1872 with bands and speeches, and brilliant illuminations of gaslight. Eight years later, around midnight on September 8, 1880, a fire started in some barrels of inflammable material. It roved through the wooden market stalls and their contents. When the fire was finally put out on the following evening, arson was suspected. Only "a block of ashes, twisted beams and tottering walls represented the finest market house in America," reported the *New York Times*. It stood almost precisely where a present-day clutter of old railroad sidings and sagging loading platforms may be swept away when a huge new convention center is constructed for the City of New York.

Fig. 16. Manhattan Market.

ILLUSTRATIONS

OF

IRON ARCHITECTURE,

MADE BY

THE ARCHITECTURAL IRON WORKS OF THE CITY OF NEW YORK.

NEW YORK:

BAKER & GODWIN, PRINTERS,

PRINTING-HOUSE SQUARE.

1865.

IRON ARCHITECTURE:

ITS ORIGIN, ADVANTAGES, AND VARIETY.

——————•—◆—•——————

THE ARCHITECTURAL IRON WORKS OF THE CITY OF NEW YORK,

The publishers of this volume, in presenting it to the public, consider it not inappropriate to give a brief account of the introduction of Iron Architecture in this country, setting forth, at the same time, some of the reasons for the superiority of Iron as a building material, and enumerating some of the many forms and uses to which it has been already applied.

It is well known that Iron has been used in England and other European countries for *interior* supports in various kinds of edifices, in the form of columns, beams, etc.; but its introduction for the *exterior* of buildings is believed to be of purely *American* invention, and of very recent origin.

The first person who practically used Iron as a building material for the exterior was Daniel D. Badger, the President of the Architectural Iron Works.

In the year 1842, Mr. Badger erected, in the city of Boston, the first structure of Iron ever seen in America. The columns and lintels of the first story were of this material, but the prevailing prejudice against this bold innovation was so great that he was not permitted to engage in the work until he had given an ample guaranty that, if it should not prove a success, he would remove it at his own expense.

All the Iron Buildings in this country have been erected since that period, and owe their existence to that humble introduction.

During the following year, A. L. Johnson, of Baltimore, brought to the notice of Mr. Badger his invention of Rolling Iron Shutters. For the purpose of using these shutters, it became necessary to construct the first stories of stores of Iron pillars and hollow posts. At once the superiority of the "Badger Fronts" (as they were then called), in all buildings where large and attractive show windows were desirable, was universally conceded, prejudice began to yield, the manufacture increased, and step by step new and more complete and elaborate designs and improvements came into being, until at last, Iron Architecture became legitimately tested and established.

Mr. Badger transferred the manufacture from Boston to New York, but in a short time it became evident, from the increasing demand for his structures, that greater facilities for their preparation were needed, and the foundation was laid for the present extensive works of this Corporation, situated on Thirteenth and Fourteenth Streets, between Avenues B and C.

Previous to Mr. Badger's introduction of Iron as a building material for exteriors, it is well known that the late Cyrus Alger, Esq., of Boston, had, about the year 1830, made plans and contemplated the erection of an Iron Dwelling House, and that he frequently had stated his conviction of its practicability, and expressed his belief that Iron would in time be adopted as the best material for first-class buildings, on account of its durability and of the beautiful forms of which it was capable, and even upon the consideration of its economy.

It is also known that about the time of Mr. Badger's introduction of this species of building in Boston, one William V. Picket published a volume in London, which he styled " A New System of Architecture, founded on the Forms of Nature, and developing the Properties of Metals."

In the preface to that volume he considered "The Capability of Metallic Bodies for the Realization of Peculiar Beauty," and set forth the value of Iron in Civil as well as Naval Architecture, on account of its "strength, durability, non-combustion, economy of space, facility of construction, and general comfort and convenience, combined with cheapness," and stated his belief that these properties would recommend the application of Iron "in the erection of dwellings and other buildings on land."

The allusion to this work of Mr. Picket is made not for the purpose of elucidating the principles of Architecture laid down by him, for his ideas would be deemed crude at the present time, but simply with the design of showing how recently the subject was regarded as so *novel* as to be claimed as a "New System of Architecture," requiring time for its introduction. Mr. Picket's work was purely theoretical, and we claim, therefore, that for the use of Iron in a practical form the world is largely indebted to Mr. Badger, who may justly be regarded as the inventor and pioneer of Iron Architecture in this country.

That a great change has been wrought in public opinion on this subject since the year 1842 will be evident when the fact is stated that it was with extreme difficulty that owners of property could, at the outset, be induced to employ Iron; the prevalent opinion being that it could not have sufficient strength to support a superstructure unless it was cast solid, and quite as cumbrous as stone, in which case its cost would have been an insuperable objection.

But, by the perseverance of years, this objection and all others were overcome, all prejudices were removed, and to day the practicability of the use of Iron for all kinds of structures is no longer doubted, even by those who were once the most skeptical.

Among those properties of Iron which commend it to more general use as a building material we may mention the following:

STRENGTH.

The established superiority of Iron in this regard now requires no argument. We may safely affirm that no substance, available for building purposes, has such closeness of texture, or is equally capable of resisting immense pressure.

The great strength of Iron secures another requisite in building, namely :

LIGHTNESS OF STRUCTURE.

A light and ornamental edifice of Iron may safely be substituted for the cumbrous structures of other substances, and sufficient strength be secured without the exclusion of the light—which is often highly desirable both for mercantile and mechanical purposes.

Combined with this we may mention

FACILITY OF ERECTION.

Nearly all the work of an Iron structure can be previously prepared and fitted in the foundry and finishing departments, and thence transferred to the place of erection and put together with rapidity and security. In some kinds of structures the facility of erection approaches the incredible.

As has been already mentioned, Iron is capable of all forms of

ARCHITECTURAL BEAUTY.

It must be evident that whatever architectural forms can be carved or wrought in wood or stone, or other materials, can also be faithfully reproduced in iron. Besides, iron is capable of finer sharpness of outline, and more elaborate ornamentation and finish ; and it may be added that it is not so liable to disintegration, by exposure to the elements, as other substances.

To this capability of beauty we may add that of

ECONOMY OR CHEAPNESS.

The cost of highly-wrought and beautiful forms in stone or marble, executed with the chisel, is often fatal to their use ; but they may be executed in Iron at a comparatively small outlay, and thus placed within the reach of those who desire to gratify their own love of art, or cultivate the public taste.

It may also be stated that no other material is so valuable for rebuilding, as Iron always has a market value, and may be recast into new forms, and adapted to new uses. Those who study economy in building should have regard to the permanence of the structure and intrinsic value of the materials, as well as the prime cost of erection.

In an eminent degree Iron possesses the property of

DURABILITY.

It may be safely affirmed that no material employed for building has such indestructibility as Iron, and none can so successfully resist the wasting influences of the elements. It is also invaluable because of its

INCOMBUSTIBILITY.

As a resistant of fire, Iron is unequaled. Wherever it is used, the cost of insurance against fire will be materially reduced; and it must be evident that by its use a building may be made absolutely fire-proof. We shall have a better claim to be considered a civilized people when we protect ourselves from the ravages of fire as well as lightning, and erect private and public buildings which are incombustible.

Destructive conflagrations in crowded cities are often arrested by fire-proof buildings, which serve as absolute barriers to the farther progress of the devouring element.

To the catalogue of the excellencies of Iron as a building material may be added its capability of

RENOVATION.

The durability of an Iron structure is such that if it becomes defaced by exposure or age, it can easily be restored to its pristine beauty by a coating of paint, and, on account of its non-absorbent surface, at less expense than structures of wood or other materials. The color also may from time to time be changed at the will of the owner.

———

THE ILLUSTRATIONS contained in the present volume will show the manifold purposes for which Iron has been applied as a building material, and also exhibit the high degree of architectural beauty which has already been attained.

Special reference to the numerous plates will show that a large number of

FIRST-CLASS STORES

In the cities of New York, Brooklyn, Philadelphia, Boston, Baltimore, New Orleans, Charleston, Mobile, Memphis, Chicago, and in fact in all large cities and towns, have their fronts built of Iron, ornamented in the most elaborate and varied styles of Architecture—the doors and windows of which are protected by the universally approved

FIRE AND BURGLAR-PROOF IRON ROLLING SHUTTERS.

These patented Shutters have been extensively used and thoroughly tested for a period of years throughout the country.

The style of Shutters made and introduced by the Architectural Iron Works is considered superior to any other in point of construction as well as price. The gearing is simple, durable, and not liable to derangement. Reference to Plates Nos. 29, 69, and 71, will show the construction and finish in detail.

It may be added that the demand for these Shutters has been so great that this Company is provided with the most complete and elaborate machinery for their speedy manufacture.

Special attention is called to the use of iron for the construction of completely fire-proof buildings to be occupied as

MANUFACTORIES,

In which strength, solidity, light, and ornament may be combined, and where the necessity of insurance against fire may be obviated. In all large cities such buildings should abound.

On pages 4, 5, and 6, will be found representations of a building of this class, situated on Mott Street, between Broome and Spring Streets, New York. This building, which was erected for I. M. Singer & Co., is six stories in height, with basement and cellar, and is throughout completely fire-proof.

An inspection of this building is needful to give an adequate idea of the solidity of its structure, and of its peculiar fitness for a manufactory.

The protection of life and property afforded by buildings of this class is alone a sufficient warrant for the slightly increased cost of their construction.

Iron has also been successfully used in the erection of

GRAIN WAREHOUSES.

The amount of the annual losses of grain and warehouse property by fire almost transcends belief. The ordinary storehouses are built wholly or in part of wood, and from certain well-known causes are peculiarly combustible, and liable to rapid decay. Such liabilities are entirely removed by the use of Iron.

The first Iron building of this character was erected in Brooklyn, for " The United States Warehousing Company."

The diagrams on pages 60, 61, and 62 will show that this structure was intended to be used for elevating, transferring, and storing grain, and protecting it against fire.

In the building referred to, the Bins, which are cylindrical, are made like boilers, of riveted plate iron; indeed, the entire structure is absolutely fire-proof and indestructible. Besides these advantages, the grain is secured from the ravages of animals and insects, and also protected from heating by arrangements made for its drying and ventilation. This single feature of ventilation is invaluable, as it will save thousands of bushels of grain which for the want of proper cooling would have to be sent to the malter's at ruinous prices. The construction of Grain Bins of this character is secured to this Corporation by letters patent.

By reference to page 12, it will be seen that Iron has been successfully used for the building of

ARSENALS

For storing Arms and Ammunition. The first building of this kind was erected in West Troy, in 1858. Safety and durability were the considerations which led to its construction, and it may safely be added that it is admirably adapted for its purposes, and is considered as having secured the objects contemplated in its erection.

IRON FERRY HOUSES

Have also been constructed by the Architectural Iron Works for the Union Ferry Company of New York and Brooklyn. These structures are an ornament to the city, and supply the place of the unsightly wooden buildings formerly occupying their position, which were liable to rapid decay and destruction by fire.

IRON OIL TANKS,

Of large capacity, capable of holding hundreds of barrels each, have been constructed for the Phenix Warehousing Company of New York, for the storage of Petroleum.

These tanks, of which many are placed under one roof, are designed to prevent loss by leakage and evaporation, and to protect the oil from the perils of fire. It is believed that they are admirably fitted for all the purposes for which they were constructed.

We would call attention to the combination of

CAST AND WROUGHT-IRON BEAMS,

As shown in PLATE LXIII. The great strength and elasticity of these Beams consist in their peculiar shape, the necessary quantity of iron being in the proper place, and the Wrought-Iron Tension-rod in the best position to sustain heavy burdens.

This is believed to be the only Beam which prevents all oscillation or trembling of the floors in buildings used for heavy or rapid-running machinery.

A recent and most successful use of Iron has been made by the "Iron Blind Company," in the construction of

VENETIAN BLINDS,

Both for the outside and inside of windows.

These Blinds present a much lighter appearance to the eye than those made of wood, over which they possess several important advantages. When opened, they admit more light than wooden Venetian Blinds; when closed, they exclude the light more perfectly; they also occupy less space, are more durable, and are proof against fire. They are not liable to warpage or shrinkage, and hence will remain for a long time in working order. They are highly approved by all who have seen or used them. This Corporation has the sole right to manufacture them.

In this connection may be mentioned the use of Iron in the construction of

WINDOW SASHES,

Which, while scarcely heavier than wood (being hollow), possess the superior advantages of beauty, durability, and incombustibility. These Sashes are especially adapted to warm climates.

It would occupy a large space to enumerate all the uses to which Iron has been applied by the Architectural Iron Works, but the following may be added to those already mentioned, namely: Bridges, Roofs, Domes, Railings, Verandahs, Balustrades, Cornices, Stairways, Columns, Capitals and Arches, Window Lintels and Sills, Consoles, Brackets and Rosettes, Urns, Door and Window Guards, Lamp, Awning and Horse Posts, Patent Lights and Iron Sidewalks.

Reference to the Table of Contents will show numerous uses besides those already enumerated.

———◆———

This volume is published at a great cost, for the twofold purpose of supplying Architects and others with plans and details for the construction of the various parts and connections of Architectural Iron Structures, and as an advertising medium for the Architectural Iron Works; and it is designed to be presented to those who may be profited by its study, and aid in the object of extending the business of the publishers, and improving the public taste.

ILLUSTRATIONS.

XXXI. Elevations and Plans of First-story Fronts.

Nos. 50 and 51.   Arranged for two stores, with Rolling Iron Shutters.

No. 52.   "   one   "   "   "   "   "

No. 53.   Arranged for two stores, without Rolling Iron Shutters.

No. 54.   "   one store, with   "   "   "   Iron Sash, &c.

No. 55.   "   "   "   passage to lofts, all enclosed with Rolling Iron Shutters.

These designs are on the scale of one-eighth of an inch to the foot, and are intended for 25-feet lots.   They can be adapted to any sized lot.

XXXII. No. 98.   Cornice, with Buttress and Corbel.

No. 50.   Top Cornice.   (See PLATE IX, Gilsey Building.)

No. 112.   Arch and Key, with Panel, &c.   (See PLATE LIV.)

No. 115.   Tracery Arch Ornament.   (See PLATE LVIII.)

XXXIII. Elevation of First-story Front, with Basement Posts and Piers, with Section and Plan of Side-walk, showing Beams, Girders, &c.

XXXIV. Elevation and Section of Two-story Fronts.

XXXV. No. 33.   Elevation of two stories of store 98 Broadway, New York, showing Rolling Iron Shutters in first story, and Panels on face of doors.

No. 34.   Elevation of first story Nos. 117 and 119 Nassau Street, New York, showing Entrance to Lofts.

XXXVI. Designs for Four-story Fronts.

No. 42, with Pilasters and Arches.

No. 48, with Columns and Antaes and Arches.

No. 46, with Pilasters and Antaes with Arches.

All arranged with or without Rolling Iron Shutters.

XXXVII. No. 17.   Elevation of two stories, with Stone or Brick above; Posts, &c., arranged for Inside Folding Shutters.

No 18.   Elevation of Two-story Front, erected in Augusta, Ga., showing Balustrade in second story.

XXXVIII. No. 9.   Elevation of Five-story Front, erected for R. A. & G. H. Witthaus, No. 38 Barclay Street, New York.

No. 10.   Elevation of Five-story Front, in Gothic Architecture.

XXXIX. No. 106.   Elevation and section of Arch, with Key elevation and section of Pier under Arch. [See PLATE XC.

No. 110.   Elevation of section of Arch with Key.   (See PLATE XL, No. 67.)

XL. No. 67.   Elevation of First-story Front, erected in Congress Street, Boston.

No. 68.   Elevation of First-story Front, No. 267 Bowery, New York.

XLI. Window Lintels.   For sizes, &c., see Catalogue of Details.

XLII.   "   "   "   "   "   "

————◄•◆•►————

CATALOGUE OF DETAILS.

				Plate.	No.
Cornice.	Enriched Modillions.	Ornamented.....		XXIII.	95
"	130 B'way.	Enriched Modill. Dentils.		"	96
"	B'way & Grand.	" Dentils		XXXII.	98
"	Gilsey.	" Trusses		"	52
"		Plain. Dentils......		XLIV.	88

Many other designs can be made with
or without enrichments.

Console or Truss.

	Height, including caps, but exclusive of foot leaf.	Project'n.	Width.	Plate.	No.
Gilsey.......	1.4	.8	.5½	X.	85
501 Broadway.	2.6½	1.5	.6	XVI.	86
130 "	3.8	1.4	1.0	XXIII.	96
	.7	.5	.6	XLII.	71
	1.10	.9	.10	XLVII.	38
	1.7	.10½	.8	"	32
	1.7	.10½	.10	"	32
	1.4½	1.2	1.0	"	47
	1.10	1.6	1.5	similar to	47
	1.11	.10½	.8	XLVII.	34
Tiffany........	1.5	3.5	.9	"	67
Thomas........	2.6½	1.11	.6	"	53
Tiffany.......	1.8½	1.7	.8	"	46
	2.3	1.2	1.2	"	8
	2.3	1.2	1.0	"	8
Similar to No. 8, but no carved mold'g on face.	2.3	.9	.10		K
	2.3	.9	1.0		K
	2.3	.9	1.2		K
Brandreth	2.9	1.5	1.4	XLVII.	35
	2.1	.9	.6	XLVIII.	275
	2.1	.9	.8	"	275
	2.1	.9	.10	"	275
	2.1	.9	1.0	"	275
	2.1	.9	1.2	"	275
	2.6	.11	.6	"	277
	2.6	.11	.8	"	277
	1.8½	.7	.7	"	279
	1.8	.5	.7	"	279
Similar to 276..	2.4	1.2	.6		G
" " ..	2.0	1.0	.8		E
	3.0	3.0	..	XLVIII.	6
	1.4	.10	.8	LXXII.	33
	..	..	..	"	36
	2.8½	.8	.8	"	37
	1.3	.7	.7	"	39
Similar to 39...	1.4	.6	.7½	..	Q
	1.4	.10	..	..	A
	1.3	.8	..	..	B
	1.8½	.11½	.8	..	F
	1.8	.6	.5	..	D
	2.0	.9	.9	..	H
Palmer........	3.2	1.7	.8	..	I
"	3.2	1.7	.10	..	I
	2.2	1.0	1.0	..	J
	2.2	1.0	1.2	..	J
	2.2	1.0	1.4	..	J
	1.6	.6	.5	..	L

	Height, including caps, but exclusive of foot leaf.	Projection.	Width.	Pl t.	No.
Console or Truss......	1.6	.6	.6	..	L
	1.8	.4	.4	..	M
Face on front.	2.0	.5	.6	..	N
	2.0	.5	.7	..	O
	2.0	.5	.7	..	P
	1.7	1.0	.8	..	R
	1.6	1.0	.8	..	S

Many other designs and sizes.

		Plate	No.
Dentils............................		V.	119
"		VIII.	117
"		"	118
"		X.	97
"		XIII.	120
"		XVIII.	100
"		XX.	87
"		"	93
"		XXIII.	96
"		XXXII.	98

Also, other designs.

		Plate	No.
Gates..................................		XCVIII.	245
"		XCIX.	257

Also, many other designs.

		Plate	No.
Girder, Arch and Tension Rod................		LXIII.	271
" " "		"	272
" " "		"	273
" " "		"	274

		Height.	Width.	Plate	No.
Guard, Door. Lattice........		4.4½	.10	LXXVII.	131
" "		4.3½	1.1	"	131
" "		4.1½	.10	"	131
" "		3.9	1.1	"	132
" "		3.9	.11½	"	132
" "		3.9	.10	"	132
" "		3.5½	1.1	"	132
" "		3.5½	.11½	"	132
" "		3.5½	.10	"	132
" "		3.1½	.10	"	132
" "		4.3½	1.1	"	130
" "		3.9	1.1	"	141
" "		3.9	.11½	"	129
" "		3.9	.11½	"	127
" "		4.3½	1.1	"	137
" "		3.9	1.1	"	137
" "		....	....	XCI.	48
" "		....	....	"	205
" "		....	....	"	206
" " any size, with or without Border.		....	....	"	203
" "		....	....	"	204
" "		....	....	"	207

All with Square or Circular Tops or Bottoms.
Also, other designs.

Truss—see Console.

    Also, other styles.

CATALOGUE OF THE PRINCIPAL WORKS

ERECTED BY THE

ARCHITECTURAL IRON WORKS.

LOCATION.	PROPRIETOR.	ARCHITECT.	DESCRIPTION.
ALBANY, N. Y., Greene St...	Albert Blair...........	....	3 Store Fronts.
Do do N. Pearl St..	James Kidd............	....	2 "
Do do do	do	—— Smith......	42 feet 4-story Front, similar to Plate XXI.
Do do	A. Koonz..............	....	1 Store Front.
Do do	Woollett & Ogden......	....	1 "
ALEXANDRIA, La..........	....	....	Court House Portico, and Main Course.
ALEXANDRIA, Egypt........	R. H. Allen & Co......	....	Iron Storehouse.
ALLEGHANY CITY, Penn.....	Gordon & Rafferty.....	....	1 Store Front.
ATLANTA, Ga..............	I. Boutell............	....	80 feet Store Front.
Do	Beach & Root.........	....	49 " "
AUBURN, N. Y.............	J. W. Haight..........	....	1 Store Front.
Do	F. L. Griswold & Co...	....	1 "
AUGUSTA, Ga..............	T. S. Metcalf.........	....	15 Store Fronts.
Do	City Bank	....	Exterior Iron Work.
Do	Lambeck & Cooper.....	....	2-story Front. Plate XXXVII., No. 18.
BALTIMORE, Md..........	Baltimore Sun........	R. G. Hatfield......	7 Store Fronts.
Do	Canfield, Brothers & Co.	....	1 "
Do	J. King..............	J. Dixon...........	1 "
BATH, N. Y.	H. W. Perrine	M. Austin.........	1 "
Do	A. S. Howell.........	G. E. Bartlett......	1 "
BOSTON, Blackstone Street...	Ritchie & Wentworth...	....	50-feet Store Fronts.
Do do do ..	Mr. Richardson........	S. P. Fuller........	87 " sim. to Pl. XXVIII., No. 62.
Do Congress do ..	L. Ware	G. J. F. Bryant....	109 " " " XL., No. 67.
Do Court do ..	J. C. Gray	C. K. Kirby	50-feet 5-story Front. See Plate LVIII.
Do Federal do ..	Mr. Kramer..........	G. J. F. Bryant....	1 Store Front. Plate XL., No. 67.
Do Theatre Alley......	C. Merriam & Sons....	S. P. Fuller.......	5 Store Fronts. Plate XXVIII., No. 62.
Do Washington St.....	H. H. Hunnewell......	George Snell.......	5-story Front. Plate LIX.
BRANT, Canada West.......	Hegeman & Co.........	....	2 Store Fronts.
BRIDGEPORT, Conn.........	S. Sterling...........	....	1 Store Front.
Do do	R. E. Stanton..........	Lambert & Bunnell.	1 "
Do do	City Bank	do	40-feet 3-story Front.
Do do	Benham, Brothers......	do	2 Store Fronts.
BROOKLYN, N. Y	Phenix Warehouse Co..	....	42 Oil Tanks, 300 bbls. each.
Do do Atlantic St.	J. Smith..............	King & Kellum	1 Store Front.
Do do Atlantic D'k.	U. States Warehouse Co.	G. H. Johnson & Co.	Grain Warehouse, Plates LX., LXI., LXII., 107 × 125 feet. 5 stories. Fire-proof.

LOCATION.	PROPRIETOR.	ARCHITECT.	DESCRIPTION.
BROOKLYN, N. Y., Fulton St.	Mr. Williams		2 Store Fronts.
Do do do	E. Lewis		1 "
Do do do	L. J. Horton		2 "
Do do do	J. O. Whitehouse		1 "
Do do do	Smith & Jewell	G. H. Johnson	Iron Works, Fulton Mills.
Do do do	City of Brooklyn		3 Engine House Fronts.
Do do do	V. G. Hall		1 Store Front.
Do do do	W. H. Cary	King & Kellum	3 Store Fronts.
Do do do	Mr. Newman	Mr. Roberts	1 Store Front.
Do do do	J. Burroughs	King & Kellum	1 "
Do do do	J. Halsey	G. H. Johnson	Halsey Building. Plate LII.
Do do do	C. V. B. Ostrander		1 Store Front.
Do do do	Smith & Jewell	G. H. Johnson & Co.	75 feet "
Do do do	Kings County	King & Tecknitz	Iron Work, Kings Co. Court Ho.: Beams, Roof, Dome, Stairs, Sashes, Shutters, &c.
Do Hamilton Av	Smith & Jewell	G. H. Johnson	Iron Work, Atlantic Flour Mill.
Do Navy Yard	U. S. Government		" Government Stores.
Do Pierrepont Place.	A. A. Low	F. A. Petersen	47 feet Greenhouse Front.
Do do do	do	do	1 Verandah.
Do do	A. A. White	do	1 "
BUFFALO, N. Y	George Coit, Jr.		2 Store Fronts.
Do	Mr. Buckley		1 "
Do	Brown, Brothers		173 feet Front, Brown's Building.
CHARLESTON, S. C.	Dwing, Thayer & Co		1 Store Front.
Do	O. M. Cohen		1 "
Do	F. O. Fanning & Co.		1 "
Do	R. Boyce		2 "
Do	H. W. Conner		1 "
Do	Hariel, Hare & Co		3 "
Do	T. A. P. Horton		1 "
Do	A. Elfe		1 "
Do	Bancroft, Betts & Marshall		2 "
Do	L. M. Hatch		1 "
Do	W. J. Walker & Brother		2 "
Do	J. E. Spear		1 "
Do	P. O'Donnell		1 "
Do	U. S. Government		Columns Custom House.
CHICAGO, Ill	C. R. Starkweather		2 Store Fronts.
Do	A. Robbins	J. M. Van Osdell	231 feet 5-story Front. Plate LIV.
Do	J. Link	do	150 feet 5- " " VII.
Do	Lloyd and Sons	do	161 feet 5- " " XIX.
Do	F. Tuttle and others	do	158 feet 5- " " LXX.
Do	Price, Church & Co		150 feet 5- "
CUBA	F. P. Dias		Market, &c.
DETROIT, Mich	F. & C. H. Buhl		4 Store Fronts.
DUNKIRK, N. Y	E. Risley & Co		5 "
FORT LAFAYETTE	U. S. Government		Iron Work.
GEORGETOWN, S. C.	S. W. Ronguie		31 feet Store Front.
GLENHAM, N. Y	Glenham Company		1 Store Front.
GRAND RAPIDS, Mich.	J. W. Pierce		1 "
Do do	W. P. Collins		2 "
HALIFAX, N. S	W. G. Combes		4-story Front. Plate LXXIX.
Do	Mr. Bennett	C. P. Thomas	1 Store Front. " LXXVI.
Do	Duffries & Co	do	2 " " LXXVIII.
Do	Mr. Coleman	do	2 " " LXXV.
Do	Mr. Billings, Jr.	do	1 " " LXVIII.

LOCATION.	PROPRIETOR.	ARCHITECT.	DESCRIPTION.
Halifax, N. S.	Mr. Chipman	C. P. Thomas	2 Store Fronts, Plate LXXIV.
Do	Mr. Skerry	do	1 Store Front, " LXXIV.
Do	Mr. Mignowitz	do	1 " " LXXIV.
Do	Mr. Billings	do	2 Store Fronts. " LXXIV.
Do	C. C. Tropolet		3 "
Do	Mr. Roman	C. P. Thomas	2 "
Do	Mr. Scott		2 "
Havana, Cuba	Pesant, Brothers		Sugar Sheds, 143 feet long. Pl. LXXIII.
Do	Spanish Navy		Lumber Sheds, 81 × 120 feet.
High Bridge	Croton Aqueduct Dept.		Railing, High Bridge.
Lancaster, Penn	J. N. Lane & Nephews		1 Store Front.
Lockport, N. Y	N. J. Dunlap		1 "
Lynchburg, Va	J. T. Davis		1 "
Do	W. S. Ellison		1 "
Martinsville, La	Tertron, Bronsard & Co.		1 "
Matanzas, Cuba	C. A. Caruano		Columns, &c., Public Hall.
Memphis, Tenn	Mosely & Hunt		4-story Front, similar to Pl. XV., No. 7.
Do	W. B. Greenlow		2 Store Fronts. Plate XXXIII.
Do	Cooke & Co	Fletcher & Wintter.	4-story " " XLVI.
Milwaukee, Wis	H. J. Nazro & Co		2 Store Fronts.
Do	Mack, Ottinger & Co	Otto Schwartz	1 Store Front.
Do	Mahler & Wendt		2 "
Do	J. B. Martin	G. H. Johnson	160 feet 4-story Front. Plate XLVI.
Mobile, Ala	J. Emanuel		2 Store Fronts.
Do	Daniels, Elgin & Co	J. H. Giles	45 feet 4-story Front.
Do	do	do	103 feet Store Front.
Newark, N. J	Mr. Dennis	Mr. Hall	1 Store Front.
Do	J. McGregor		40 feet 4-story Front. Plate XXVI.
Do	J. W. Corey		1 Store Front.
New Haven, Conn	H. N. Whittlesey		2 Store Fronts.
Do	T. Bennett		2 "
Do	Perkins, Treat & Chatfield		2 "
Do	Young Men's Inst		2 "
Do	A. Parker		3 "
New London, Conn	S. & G. Rogers		2 "
New Orleans, La	Paul Tulane		47 feet 5-story Front. Plate VII.
Do	J. B. Lee		62 feet Store Front.
NEW YORK:			
Barclay St., No. 34	R. A. & G. Witthaus	S. A. Warner	5-story Front. Plate XXXVIII., No. 9.
Do 36, 38		T. R. Jackson	2 Store Fronts.
Do 50	Mr. Gibson	J. C. Wells	1 "
Do 52, 54	Wolfe & Mickle		2 "
Do 58	T. E. Gilbert	W. H. Hume	1 "
Beekman St., 23, 25			2 "
Do 27			1 "
Do 29	Remsen & Ely	G. W. Noble	1 "
Do 55, 57		J. B. Snook	2 " and Rears.
Do 79, 81		Do	2 "
Do 83		Do	5-story Front. Plate XC., No. 14.
Bleecker St., cor. Mercer.	Mr. Bosch		1 Store Front.
Do do	Judge Jackson	Kellum & Son	35 feet Store Front.
Do do	A. T. Stewart	J. B. Snook	82 " "
Bowery, No. 13	C. S. Hines		1 Store Front and Basement.
Do 70, 72	Wm. B. Astor		2 " "
Do 96	A. L. Ely	R. G. Hatfield	1 "
Do 98		Thomas & Son	1 "

LOCATION.	PROPRIETOR.	ARCHITECT.	DESCRIPTION.
NEW YORK:			
Bowery, No. 110	A. L. Ely	R. G. Hatfield.....	1 Store Front and Basement.
Do 163......	McGraw and Taylor....	....	1 "
Do 267......	J. B. Simpson	J. B. Snook........	1 " Plate XL., No. 68.
Do cor. Canal..	Lorillards	Thomas & Son....	132 feet Store Front.
Do " Delancey.	J. B. Simpson..........	A. Winham........	50 "
Do " Houston.	Lorillards....	....	4 Store Fronts.
Do " Bond...	....	J. B. Snook	40 feet "
Bridge St................	R. Blanco..............	....	91 " "
Broadway, Nos. 39 to 49....	McCurdy, Aldrich & Spencer.................	....	5 Store Fronts.
Do 53.........	P. & R. Goelet	....	5-story Front and Basem't. Pl. XV., No. 8.
Do 61.........	....	S. A. Warner......	82 feet Store Front.
Do 63, 65......	L. S. Suarez..........	....	2 Store Fronts.
Do 70.........	James Harriot & Co....	....	1 Store Front.
Do 72.........	Mr. Cruger...........	Thomas & Son.....	1 "
Do 84.........	Mr. St. John	R. G. Hatfield	31 feet Front, 2 story. Pl. XXXV., No.33.
Do 102........	Continental Ins. Co.....	G. Thomas........	2 Store Fronts.
Do 112, 114....	Bowen & McNamee	....	Patent Shutters for 2 Fronts.
Do 130........	W. H. Hume.........	W. H. Hume......	5-story Front. Plate XXII.
Do 139........	....	J. F. Duckworth...	1 Store Front.
Do 141........	G. & W. Young	....	1 "
Do 151........	....	J. F. Duckworth...	1 "
Do 156, 158....	D. H. Haight.........	J. B. Snook	2 Store Fronts.
Do 161, 163, 165.	F. Marquand.........	....	3 "
Do 177........	W. H. Smith	....	1 Store Front.
Do 179........	Thomas Hunt	King & Kellum....	1 "
Do 187........	Noel J. Becar.........	....	1 "
Do 194........	L. M. Wiley.........	....	1 "
Do 199........	—— Young.........	....	1 "
Do 202........	A. Cleveland	Thomas & Son.....	1 "
Do 203........	J. Q. Jones..........	....	1 "
Do 204........	Appletons............	Thomas & Son.....	1 "
Do 205........	W. H. Smith	....	1 " and Basement.
Do 235........	Tracy, Irwin & Co......	Thomas & Son	1 "
Do 241, 243....	Solomon & Hart	F. A. Petersen.....	2 Store Fronts.
Do 245........	D. O'Connor ..;.......	....	1 Store Front.
Do 252........	....	....	5-story Front, similar to Plate XV., No. 7.
Do 257........	Mr. Field	....	1 Store Front.
Do 287........	S. Storms	....	1 "
Do 292, 296....	J. De Forest	....	2 Store Fronts.
Do 294........	B. Pike, Jr..........	....	1 Store Front.
Do 300........	W. B. Astor..........	G. Thomas	1 "
Do 306........	Mr. Barclay..........	....	1 "
Do 332........	John Dolan	J. B. Snook........	5-story Front, similar to Plate XC.
Do 341........	Paton & Co...........	J. H. Giles........	1 Store Front.
Do 343........	Geo. Ponsot..........	....	1 "
Do 349........	J. & I Cox	....	1 "
Do 355........	Adriance & Strang.....	....	1 "
Do 360........	P. Lorillard..........	....	1 "
Do 361, 363....	H. Wood.............	J. Rogers..........	2 Store Fronts. [No. 66.
Do 369........	Solomon & Hart.......	F. A. Petersen.....	1 Store Front and Basement. Pl. XXVIII.,
Do 371, 375....	Dr. Moffat	....	2 " " and Rear.
Do 372........	H. D. Aldrich	S. A. Warner......	1 "
Do 373........	L. Spencer	J. B. Snook........	5-story Front and Basement. Plate XIX.
Do 377, 379....	Mr. Lawrence	....	2 Store Fronts.

LOCATION.		PROPRIETOR.	ARCHITECT.	DESCRIPTION.
NEW YORK:				
Broadway, No. 388		D. Wood	King & Kellum	1 Store Front, Basement and Rear.
Do	403	P. & R. Goelet		1 "
Do	404, 406, 408	P. Lorillard		3 Store Fronts.
Do	405	Duncan & Sons		1 Store Front.
Do	442 to 454	G. W. Miller	A. Winnam	125 feet Store Fronts. City Assembly R'ms.
Do	447	Mr. Collamore		1 Store Front.
Do	449	Mr. Jackson		1 "
Do	452, 454	Peter Goelet		1 "
Do	456	T. Woodruff		1 "
Do	471	W. Gibson		1 "
Do	481	J. De Wolfe		1 "
Do	495	Grover & Baker	G. H. Johnson	3-story Front. Plate XI.
Do	501	O. B. Potter	Thomas & Son	5-story Front. Sim. to Plate XC.
Do	502, 504	Dr. H. Bostwick	Kellum & Son	2-store Fronts. Basement and Rear.
Do	506	E. Langdon		1 Store Front.
Do	508			1 "
Do	516	Savings Bank		Pat. Shutters for Front
Do	535	S. Brewster		1 store Front.
Do	543	W. B. Astor		1 "
Do	547			1 "
Do	550	Tiffany & Co	R. G. Hatfield	1 " and Base't. Plate LXIV., No. 26.
Do	552, 554	R. French	J. B. Snook	2 "
Do	555	A. R. Eno	Thomas & Son	1 "
Do	577, 579, 581	Langdon family		3 "
Do	585		J. Rogers	1 "
Do	601	W. & E. Mitchell		1 "
Do	604			1 "
Do	606			1 "
Do	620	Henry Dolan	J. B. Snook	6-story Front. Sim. to Plate VII.
Do	621	Gerard Stuyvesant		1 Store Front.
Do	624, 626	Uhl & Whitney	J. M. Trimble	Ent. to L. Keene's Thea. Pl. LXIV., No. 24.
Do	627, 629	S. Brewster		2 Store Fronts.
Do	631 to 637	P. & R. Goelet		4 "
Do	645	Mr. Agate		1 Store Front.
Do	653		J. F. Duckworth	1 "
Do	654			1 "
Do	667 to 677	J. La Farge	Jas. Renwick	150 ft " Old La Farge House.
Do	"	"	Jas. Renwick	150 ft " New " "
Do	679			1 "
Do	701	Mr. Manice		1 "
Do	706			1 "
Do	711	Mr. Holmes		1 "
Do	747	J. G. Pearson		1 "
Do	752	N. Y. Dyeing & P. Est.		1 "
Do	758	S. Kohnstamm	Kellum & Son	1 "
Do	785	J. Colles		1 "
Do	845	C. V. S. Roosevelt		1 "
Do	847	"		1 "
Do	cor Exch. Pl.	J. Steward, Jr., & Co		1 "
Do	" Pine	Continental Ins. Co.	Thomas & Son	2 Fronts.
Do	" Cedar		J. B. Snook	2 store Fronts.
Do	" Liberty	Mr. Herrick		1 Store Front.
Do	" Cortlandt			1 "
Do	" "	P. Gilsey	J. W. Ritch	6-story Front. 163 ft. Gilsey Build., Pl. IX.
Do	" Dey	W. W. Chester		1-store Front.

LOCATION.		PROPRIETOR.	ARCHITECT.	DESCRIPTION.
NEW YORK:				
Broadway, cor. Murray		Ball, Tompkins & Black		1 Store Front.
Do	" Warren	S. V. Hoffman	J. B. Snook	Pat. Shutters, 150 feet Front.
Do	" Chamber and Reed.	A. T. Stewart	J. B. Snook	"
Do	" Pearl	J. Gemmell	S. A. Warner	50 feet Store Front.
Do	" Anthony	Dr. J. Moffat		1 Store Front.
Do	" Pearl&Worth	J. R. Whiting	Kellum & Son	175 feet Store Front and Basement.
Do	" Leonard	Appletons		2 Store Fronts.
Do	" "			1 "
Do	" "	W. G. Lane & Co		198 feet Store Front.
Do	" Franklin	W. Gibson		1 Store Front.
Do	" "	John Taylor	Thomas & Son	75 feet Front. Taylor's Saloon.
Do	" White	Mr. Clark		1 Store Front.
Do	" Canal and Lispenard	Dr. Brandreth	Chas. Mettam	290 feet Store Front and main cornice. Brandreth House.
Do	" Grand	B. Wood	R. G. Hatfield	130 feet Store Front.
Do	" Broome	W. Gale & Son	Chas. Mettam	228 ft. "
Do	" "	W. Langdon	J. P. Gaynor	5-story Front. 162 ft. Haughwout Building Plate III.
Do	" Spring	R. H. Haight & Co .,	J. B. Snook	470 ft. " St. Nicholas Hotel.
Do	" "	J. J. Astor's heirs	R. G. Hatfield & D. Lemon.	176 ft. "
Do	" Prince	A. T. Stewart	Trench & Snook	237 ft. " Metropolitan Hotel.
Do	" Fourth	Mr. Philbin		113 ft. "
Do	" Wash'ton Pl.			35 ft. " 2 story.
Do	" Ninth street			1 Store Front.
Do	" Tenth	J. Beck	R. Henry	163 ft. " 2 story.
Do	" Twelfth	S. Whitney's heirs		2 Store Fronts and Basements.
Do	" Thirteenth	Mr. Valentine		58 ft. "
Do	" Twentieth			1 Store Front.
Do	" Twenty-first	S. Halsted	King & Kellum	2 " Pl. XXIV. No. 64.
Do	" Madison Sq			2 "
Do	" Twenty-fifth	Mr. Livingston	J. B. Snook	2 "
Do	bet. 25th and 26th	S. V. Hoffman	J. B. Snook	Hoffman Hotel.
Do	cor. Twenty-sixth.	Mr. Dodworth	Renwick & Co	142 ft. Front.
Do		Mr. Bulkley		1 Store Front.
Do		W. Snickner		1 "
Do		S. Brewster		3 "
Do				1 "
Burling Slip		A. A. Low		2 Store Fronts.
Canal street, 253		J. Hesley	Kellum & Son	1 " and Basement.
Do	262	P. H. Frost		1 "
Do	cor Wooster	Rosenblat & Banta	W. T. Beers	2 "
Do	" Thompson	People's Bank	Thomas & Son	75 ft. "
Do		Mr. White		1 Store Front.
Do		N. & J. Brown		1 "
Do				1 "
Cedar		J. D .Phillips		2 story Front.
Central Park		C. P. Commissioners	Olmstead & Vaux	Bridge Railing. Plate XC., No. 229.
Chambers Street :				
Do	43 to 49	Spencer, Wyeth&Stewart	R. Henry	4 Store Fronts and Rear.
Do	53	R. Henry		1 " "
Do	76		J. M. Rich	1 "
Do	77	Peddie & Merriam		5-story Front and Basement, similar to Plate XXXVIII, No. 39.

LOCATION.	PROPRIETOR.	ARCHITECT.	DESCRIPTION.
NEW YORK:			
Chambers Street, 78	Dr. Alcock		1 Store Front.
Do 80, 82	Mr. Holmes		2 "
Do 88			1 "
Do 113			1 " and Basement.
Do 120	W. H. Jones		50 ft. Store Front, 5-story, sim. to Pl. XC.
Do 122			1 Store Front and Basement.
Do 126, 128	Holmes & Colgate	Thomas & Son	2 "
Do 152			1 " and Basement.
Do cor Church	T. Suffern		45 ft. "
Do and Warren	H. D. Aldrich	S. A. Warner	2 Store Fronts.
Do " Reade	A. T. Stewart	J. B. Snook	218 ft. " and Basement.
Do " "	J. Haggerty		2 Store Fronts.
Do " "	W. S. Wetmore		240 ft. Front.
Do " "	W. H. Cary	King & Kellum	100 " 5-story. Pl. VII.
Chatham Street, 19	J. B. Simpson	J. B. Snook	1 Store Front. Basement and Rear.
Do 65	Chatham Bank	J. B. Snook	1 "
Do 74			1 "
Do	J. B. & W. Simpson		2 " French's Hotel.
Church Street,	S. D. Babcock	T. S. Wall	1 "
"	Mr. Matthews		1 "
" cor Fulton	Mr. Phyfe	J. B. Snook	108 ft. "
Cliff Street, 22	Mr. James		1 Store Front and Rear.
College Place, 7	W. H. Grinnell	R. H. Mook	5-story " and Base't. Pl. XV, No. 7.
Cortlandt Street 3	C. & U. J. Smith		1 Store "
Do 4	C. Vanderbilt		1 "
Do 6, 8	Brown & Cushing		2 "
Do 12, 14, 16		Mr. Hurry	3 "
Do 15, 17	Mr. Dwire		2 "
Do 18			1 "
Do 19, 21			2 "
Do 20	Gilbert, Prentiss & Tuttle		1 "
Do 22	Bennett & Johnson		1 "
Dey Street, 5, 7	Noel J. Becar		2 "
Do 13	Wilson & Co		1 "
Do 15	Mr. Cox		1 "
Do 44	E. H. Main		1 "
Do 46			1 "
Duane Street, 42	Archl. Iron Works	G. H. Johnson	5-story " and Base. Sim. to Pl. VII.
Do 68, 75 to 85	Mr. Palmer	J. B. Snook	165 ft. " 5-story. Sim. to Pl. XIX.
Do 71, 73	J. B. Snook	J. B. Snook	50 ft. " and Basement.
Do 84,		J. F. Duckworth	5-story " and Basement.
Do 116			1 Store Front and Basement.
Do and Reade			2 "
Do cor Church	Dr. Lovejoy	Amzi Hill	116 ft. "
Do " Reade	East River Bank		1 Store Front.
FifthAv. 23d St, B'way&24th	A. R. Eno	Thomas & Son	277 ft. Front. Fifth Avenue Hotel.
Fourth Av	Harlem Railroad Co		Columns, &c., Engine Depot.
Do cor 23d Street		Mettam & Burke	5 Store Fronts.
Franklin Street, 73	John Mack	Renwick & Co	1 " Pl. XCII.
Do 91	"	"	1 "
Do cor Franklin Pl		Thomas & Son	53 ft. " Basement and Rear.
Do " Church	W. Watson	T. S. Wall	2 Store Fronts.
Do "	"	"	2 "
Front Street	J. K. & E. B. Place	E. L. Roberts	1 "
" 166			1 "

LOCATION.	PROPRIETOR.	ARCHITECT.	DESCRIPTION.
NEW YORK:			
Fulton Street, 58, 60........	....	....	2 Store Fronts.
Do 115..........	....	....	1 "
Do 141..........	M. Reily............	....	1 "
Do 186..........	J. Tucker...........	....	1 "
Do 198..........	Mr. Phyfe...........	....	1 "
Do	Union Ferry Co........	Kellum & Son.....	Fulton Ferry House.
Gouverneur's Lane........	E. Banker & Co........	....	3 Store Fronts.
Grand Street, cor. Chrystie..	Lord & Taylor........	Thomas & Son....	200 ft. "
Do " Allen.....	Mr. Donnelly..........	T. S. Wall........	1 Store Front.
Greenwich Street, 52.......	....	Griffiths..........	1 "
Do 218.......	....	C. Mettam........	1 "
Do 282.......	....	Thomas & Son....	1 "
Do	A. T. Lagrave........	....	1 "
Do	Mr. Platt............	....	1 "
Do	W. B. Astor..........	....	1 "
Howard Street,...........	....	....	1 "
Hudson St. 250...........	Mr. Sloan...........	....	1 "
Do 277, 279, 281....	B. Newhouse........	....	3 "
Do 297...........	A. M. L. Scott........	....	1 "
Do cor Broome......	J. S. Hasbrook.......	....	1 "
Do " Jay........	Am. Express Co........	J. W. Ritch.......	204 ft. "
Irving Pl., " 15th........	Manhattan Gas Co......	W. W. Gardiner...	1 Office Front.
John St., 19............	F. W. Lasak..........	....	1 Store Front.
Do 20............	Mr. Young...........	....	1 "
Do 22............	....	....	1 "
Do 75............	J. K. Herrick........	F. Diaper........	1 "
Leonard St.,71............	....	S. A. Warner......	1 "
Do 73............	....	J. F. Duckworth....	1 "
Do 80............	Paton & Co.........	J. H. Giles........	1 "
Do 84............	Mr. Sniffin..........	....	1 " and Basement.
Liberty St., 25, 27.........	W. B. Windle........	....	1 "
Do 29............	F. W. Lasak.........	....	1 "
Do 85............	....	....	1 "
Do 93............	J. M. Matthews.......	....	1 "
Do 95, 97..........	Murphy & Benedict.....	....	2 "
Do 96............	Mr. McBride.........	....	1 "
Do 99............	A. R. Eno...........	....	1 "
Do 103...........	T. Strang...........	....	1 "
Do 105...........	J. J. Henry..........	....	1 "
Do	....	J. B. Snook.......	1 " and Basement.
Ludlow St., near Houston...	....	H. Fernback......	4 "
Do	B. R. Winthrop.......	....	1 "
Madison Av..............	....	....	Columns—Ch. of Incarnation.
Maiden Lane 2............	W. H. Smith.........	....	1 Store Front.
Do 4............	Mr. Young...........	....	1 "
Do 6............	W. H. Smith.........	....	1 "
Do 8............	....	....	1 "
Do 9, 11, 13,.......	Swan & Co..........	....	3 "
Do 10............	....	....	1 "
Do 15 and 25.......	W. H. Smith.........	....	2 "
Do 17, 19.........	J. Fellowes & H. Young.	....	2 " and Rears.
Do 21, 23.........	Fellowes & Schell......	....	2 "
Do 22............	J. E. Hyde's Sons......	....	1 "
Do 31............	....	....	1 "
Do 33............	P. Murray...........	....	1 "

LOCATION.		PROPRIETOR.	ARCHITECT.	DESCRIPTION.
NEW YORK:				
MaidenLane,	35	L. Murray		1 Store Front.
Do	38			1 "
Do	47			1 "
Do	51 to 61	A. H. Wood		5 Store Fronts.
Do	56	W. B. Windle	J. B. Snook	1 "
Do	58			1 " and Basement.
Do	63	R. Mortimer		1 "
Do	123	R. & N. Dart		1 "
Do	cor. Little Green.	Platt Bros		1 "
Do	" "	W. H. Smith		3 "
Do	" Nassau	Est. of J. Duidam		39 feet "
Mercer St.,	5, 7		J. B. Snook	2 Store Fronts.
Do	18	A. T. Stewart	Kellum & Son	5-story Front and Basement.
Do	cor Howard	A. R. Eno		1 Store Front.
Do	Rear 555 B'way.	John Taylor		1 Store Rear.
Do		W. Gibson		1 Store Front.
Mott St.,		I. M. Singer & Co	G. H. Johnson	Sewing Machine Manfy. Pl. IV. and VI.
Murray St.,	6			1 Store Front.
Do	8, 10	E. Parmly		2 "
Do	14	J. L. Platt		1 "
Do	16	O. Thompson		1 "
Do	17 to 29	H. D. Aldrich	S. A. Warner	7 "
Do	36	Dr. Scott		1 "
Do	37, 39	A. Higgins		2 "
Do	41		Thomas & Son	1 "
Do	45	Mr. Hutchings	S. A. Warner	1 "
Do	46		S. A. Warner	1 "
Do	47	W. Sturtevant	J. C. Wells	1 "
Do	49			1 "
Do	55			1 "
Do	cor College Pl.	Mr. Stevens		189 ft. "
Do				1 Store Front.
Do		Dr. Hunter		1 "
Nassau St.,	33			1 "
Do	52, 54	C. & U. J. Smith		2 "
Do	115 to 121	N. C. Platt	J. Sexton	4 " and Rears, Pl. XXXV. No.34
Do	cor Maiden Lane.	Mr. Swan		2 "
Do		Mr. Taylor		1 "
Do		Mr. Youngs		1 "
New William St.,	10	W. H. Smith		1 "
Park Place	3	F. Pares	King & Kellum	1 Store Front and Basement.
Do	9, 11	E. Parmly		2 "
Do	12	Judge Roosevelt		1 "
Do	17	J. L. Platt		1 "
Do	19	O. Thompson		1 "
Do	21	E. B. Strange		1 "
Do	Church & Barclay	C. W. & J. T. Moore	Thomas & Son	147 ft. "
Do	College Pl. & Barclay	Chittenden, Bliss & Co.	S. A. Warner	138 ft. "
Do	and Murray	Lathrop & Ludington	"	117 ft. "
Do	cor. Church	Wm. Watson		167 ft. "
Do	"	W. G. Hunt & Co	King & Kellum	145 ft. "
Do	" College Pl.	Thomas Hunt	"	150 ft. "
Do		E. Parmly		1 Store Front.
Do		D. B. St. John		2 "
Do		Christie & Constant		1 " and Basement.

LOCATION.	PROPRIETOR.	ARCHITECT.	DESCRIPTION.
NEW YORK:			
Park Place................	T. Slocum...............	....	100 ft. Front.
Do	Spofford & Tileston.....	....	2 Store "
Park Row, 13, 15..........	Mr. Bangs..............	....	2 "
Do	W. B. Astor & J. J. Phelps.	Thomas & Son.....	5 "
Pearl St., 282.............	H. V. Hendrick........	....	1 "
Do	W. H. Cary...........	King & Kellum....	2 "
Do	Mary Chesebrough.......	"	1 " and Basement.
Do	M. Halsted.............	"	1 "
Do	J. H. Coster...........	"	1 "
Do	R. Carmley.............	"	1 "
Do	P. Williams............	"	1 "
Do	L. G. Morris..........	"	1 "
Do	....	"	38 ft. "
Do cor. Moore......	....	....	1 Store Front.
Peck Slip, " Front......	J. S. Harris & Co.......	R. G. Hatfield.....,	103 ft. Front.
Pine St., 11..........	A. J. Cipriant........	....	2-story Front.
Reade St., 74.............	Mr. Bradshaw..........	....	1 Store Front.
Do 97, 99, 101......	A. Higgins............	J. F. Duckworth...	3 "
Do 103...........	Gilbert Estate..........	....	1 " and Rear on Chambers St.
Do 104.............	....	....	1 "
Do cor. Church.....	Read & Bradshaw.......	G. H. Giles........	86 ft. " and Basement.
Do " "	....	Kellum & Son.....	160 ft. " "
Do	Bliss, Briggs & Douglas.	S. A. Warner......	100 ft. "
Do	R. H. McCurdy........	....	50 ft. " and basement.
Do	J. Q. Jones...........	....	5-story " Pl. XV., No. 8.
Sixth Avenue, No. 206	G. P. Rogers...........	....	1 Store Front.
Third " 805	....	W. T. Beers.......	1 "
Third Ave., cor. 34th St	H. Hughes.............	do	56 feet Store Front.
Third and Fourth Av., Astor			[Inside Cast Iron Work.
Place and Seventh St.....	Peter Cooper..........	F. A. Petersen.....	326 ft. Store Front, Cooper Inst., and all
Twenty-fourth Street	A. R. Eno.............	....	Fifth Avenue Hotel Front.
University Place	Society Library	Thomas & Son.....	Main Cornice & Balust'de. Pl. XX., No. 93.
Vesey St., No. 22	W. Morris.............	....	1 Store Front.
Do 36.........	S. Sutton.............	....	1 "
Do 45.........	J. Osborn	....	1 "
Do	S. Sutton	....	50 ft. Store F'nt, 5-story, sim. to Pl. LVIII.
Walker St., No. 24.........	M. H. Litchstein.......	King & Kellum....	1 Store Front and Basement.
Do 36........	T. Lewis..............	....	1 "
Do 38........	Mr. Lewis.............	....	1 "
Do 44........	G. Johnson...........	Thomas & Son.....	1 "
Do 48, 50.....	Mr. Lane.............	R. G. Hatfield	2 " [XV., No. 7.
Do 61........	Mrs. Goelet...........	....	5-story Front and Basement, similar to Pl.
Do	J. Lee...............	Kellum & Son	5 " " " sim. to Pl. CII.
Wall St., Nos. 8 to 20......	J. G. Pearson and others.	J. G. Pearson	6 Store Fronts, 2-story, similar to Plate XXXVII., No. 17.
Do 49	....	....	1 Store Front.
Do	Mechanics' Bank.......	R. Upjohn & Co....	Dome and Lantern, 126 feet circumference.
Warren St., Nos. 4, 6	S. V. Hoffman	....	2 Store Fronts.
Do 8........	A. M. Lyon...........	....	1 "
Do 11........	J. Lee...............	R. G. Hatfield......	1 "
Do 12, 14	A. Higgins...........	....	2 "
Do 15........	F. E. Gilbert.........	....	1 "
Do 16........	T. March............	....	1 "
Do 17, 19.....	Henrys, Smith & Townsend.............	....	2 "
Do 18, 20.....	Mr. Cleveland........	....	2 "

LOCATION.	PROPRIETOR.	ARCHITECT.	DESCRIPTION.
NEW YORK:			
Warren Street, 23, 25	C. A. Bandouine	Mr. Gardiner	51 ft. Store Front.
Do 24	Mr. Martin		1 "
Do 26, 28, 30	Allan, McComb & Langlois		3 "
Do 37, 39	T. U. Smith & J. J. Henry		2 "
Do 38			1 "
Do 40	C. A. Bandouine	Mr. Gardiner	1 "
Do 41, 43	T. Suffern	J. W. Ritch	2 "
Do 42	J. A. Stevens		1 "
Do 49	Rogers & Walker	S. A. Warner	1 "
Do 51	Mr. Center		1 "
Do 53	F. E. Gilbert		1 "
Do 55	Judge Whiting		1 "
Do 76	Mrs. P. Bonnet	Thomas & Son	1 "
Do cor. Church	H. D. Aldrich	S. A. Warner	2 "
Water St., No. 120	A. Hendricks		1 "
White do 79	S. Kohnstamm	Thomas & Son	1 " [Pl. CII.
Do cor. Franklin Pl.	S. H. & J. E. Condict	Kellum & Son	73 ft. " 5-story, Basement and Rear,
Whitehall St.	Union Ferry Co	J. Kellum	South and Hamilton Ferry Houses.
Do	Corn Exchange	E. L. Roberts	Iron Work Corn Exchange.
William St., No. 93	A. H. Ward		1 Store Front.
Do 128			1 "
Do 130	A. B. & D. Sands		1 "
Do 163	B. A. Field		1 "
Do cor. Ann	S. N. Livingston		1 "
Do	Great Western Ins. Co.	Renwick & Sands	Insurance Building.
Worth St.		S. A. Warner	315 feet Store Front and Basement.
Do No. 39		J. F. Duckworth	1 Store Front.
Do 41		J. F. Duckworth	"
Do 43, 45	Mr. Nesmith	S. A. Warner	50 ft. "
OSWEGO, N. Y	Oswego Hotel Co	W. T. Beers	300 feet Front.
Do	T. Kingsford & Son		Oswego Starch Factory.
PANAMA	Panama Railroad Co		Railroad Depot.
Do	do		Verandah, &c.
PETERBORO', C. W	R. Nicholls		2 Store Fronts. Plate XXVIII., No. 65.
PETERSBURG, Va	D. A. Paul		1 Store Front.
Do	Lyon, Abraham & Davis		1 "
PHILADELPHIA:			
Arch St., No. 116	Jones, White & Oo		1 "
Do 124	W. H. Hart		1 "
Chestnut St., 49	A. Masson		1 "
Do 51	do		1 "
Do 52	J. A. Gendell		1 "
Do 54	W. W. Keen		1 "
Do 56	J. A. Gendell		1 "
Do 61	do		1 "
Do 63	do		1 "
Do 65	Mr. Landreth		1 "
Do 85	Mr. Lewis		1 "
Do 87	do		1 "
Do 115	W. W. Keen		1 "
Do 123	S. H. Hoxie		1 "
Do 136	Bailey & Co		1 "
Do	J. F. Fisher		3 Store Fronts.
Do	Dr. Swaim		3 " Swaim's Building.
Do	Jules Harrel		1 Store Front.

LOCATION.	PROPRIETOR.	ARCHITECT.	DESCRIPTION.
PHILADELPHIA :			
Chestnut St	Mr. Dunbar............	....	2 Store Fronts. Pl. XXIV., No. 25.
Do	Girard Estate..........	....	2 " Girard Buildings.
Do	Williamson & Mellor...	....	3 " Pl. LXIV., No. 25.
Do	A. Foit...............	....	1 Store Front.
Commerce St..........	C. C. Cope...........	....	1 "
Lodge Alley	Williamson & Mellor...	....	3 Store Fronts.
Do	Mr. Dunbar...........	....	2 "
Market St., No. 81....	C. H. Fisher..........	....	1 Store Front.
Do 147....	M. L. Hollowell........	....	Rolling Shutters for Front.
North Third St........	Mr. Madora..........	....	1 Store Front.
Sixth St..............	D. Landrith	....	2 Store Fronts.
South Fourth St.......	R. T. Shepherd........	....	2 "
Do	W. Ford	....	1 Store Front.
Do	J. A. Gendell.........	....	3 Store Fronts.
Strawberry St.........	W. W. Keen..........	....	2 "
Third St..............	Mr. Ballinger	....	2 " Pl. XXXV., No. 34.
Do	Mr. Fassit	....	1 Store Front.
Do	Siegur, Lamb & Co.....	....	1 "
Do	Faust & Wineburne....	....	1 "
Do	Mr. Stone............	....	1 "
Do	Towns & Sharpless.....	....	1 " 2 stories.
Washington Ave.......	Penn. Railroad Co.....	G. H. Johnson.....	Grain Warehouse. Plates LX., LXI., LXII. 107 × 125 ft. 5 stories. Fire-proof.
PITTSBURG, Penn...........	Mr. Yeager	....	1 Store Front.
Do	A. A. Mason & Co	....	1 "
Do	C. H. Paulson.........	....	2 Store Fronts.
Do	J. Brown.............	....	2 " sim. to Pl. XXXV., No. 34.
PITTSFIELD, Mass...........	J. C. West...........	....	3 "
Do	Plumpkit & Hartbut ...	....	1 Store Front.
PORTLAND, Me............	H. N. Jose...........	....	2 Store Fronts.
PROVIDENCE, R. I..........	G. A. Howard.........	....	475 feet Store Fronts.
Do	Tolman & Bucklin.....	....	5 Store Fronts.
Do	Wm. Andrews.........	....	2 "
Do	Mr. Duncan..........	....	8 "
Do	S. Dexter............	....	2 "
Do	B. D. Wheedon.......	....	2 "
Do	H. Rogers...........	....	2 "
Do	J. Arnold............	....	4 "
RICHMOND, Va............	Stebbing, Darricott & Co....	....	3 "
Do	W. Barrett...........	....	5 "
Do	Kent, Payne & Kent ...	....	2 "
Do	J. P. Ballard.........	....	1 Store Front.
Do	O. A. Stryker	....	Rolling Shutters for Front.
RIO JANEIRO, Brazil.......	Dr. T. Rainey	J. Whyte..........	Ferry Ho., 100 ft. Front. Pl. LXXXVIII.
ROCHESTER, N. Y	Elwanger & Barry	....	75 feet Store Front.
Do	Mr. Erricson..........	....	86 " "
Do	W. A. Reynolds........	....	58 " "
Do	Samuel Wilder	....	1 Store Front.
Do	D. W. Powers	....	1 "
ROME, N. Y..............	Hill, Brothers & Co....	....	1 "
SACRAMENTO, Cal..........	....	....	1 "
SAN FRANCISCO, Cal........	R. M. Sherman........	....	2 Store Fronts.
Do	G. R. Jackson & Co....	....	1 Store Front.
Do	J. B. Snook	J. B. Snook........	2 Store Fronts.
Do	....	....	118 feet Store Front.

LOCATION.	PROPRIETOR.	ARCHITECT.	DESCRIPTION.
SAN FRANCISCO, Cal........	....	....	34 feet Store Front.
SAVANNAH, Ga............	S. C. Deming..........	....	2 Store Fronts.
SCRANTON, Penn..........	Mr. Shopland..........	....	1 Store Front.
SHARON SPRINGS, N. Y.....	....	L. Burgher	Pavillion over Spring.
SPRINGFIELD, Mass........	Foot & Co.............	....	4 Store Fronts.
Do	.... D. W. Barnes..........	A. L. Chapin.......	1 Store Front.
Do	.... John Madden..........	....	1 "
STAMFORD, Conn..........	Augustus Weed........	M. B. Wolsey......	38 feet Store Front and Balcony.
SYRACUSE, N. Y..........	Dillaye, Brothers.......	....	3 Store Fronts.
TROY, N. Y..............	H. E. & W. Allendorph.	....	1 Store Front.
Do	.... Jacobs & Caswell	....	1 "
Do	.... Troy City Bank	....	38 feet Store Front.
Do	.... L. Smith............	King & Tecknitz...	1 Store Front.
TROY, Penn..............	E. W. Perrine.........	....	1 "
UTICA, N. Y.............	J. Sayer	....	1 "
VICKSBURG, Miss..........	J. B. Wheeler & Co....	....	1 " [XII.
WATERVLIET, N. Y	U. S. Government......	....	Arsenal Storehouse, 100 by 196 feet. Pl.
Do	do	....	Arsenal. Iron Work.
WASHINGTON, D. C.........	do	....	Extension Congressional Library.
Do	do	....	Patent Iron Lathing Extension, Treasury
Do	do	....	Iron Work, Ford's Theatre. [Build'g.
WILMINGTON, N. C.........	W. A. Barry..........	....	1 Store Front.

VIEW OF THE ARC

13ᵀᴴ & 14ᵀᴴ S

ARCHITECTURAL
IRON WORKS
D.D.BADGER & C?
FOUNDRY &
MACHINE SHOP

ARCHITECTURAL IRON WORKS

OFFICE 42 DUANE ST.

MANUFACTURERS OF IRON BUILDINGS &c.

AVENUE C.

OFFICE

ARCHITECTURAL
IRON
WORKS
14 ? S? & AV? C.

Lith. 449 Broadway New York.

TECTURAL IRON WORKS

AST RIVER, NEW YORK.

Plate III

No:30.

ARCHITECTURAL IRON WORKS,— NEW-YORK.

Plate IV.

Nº 15.

Front Elevation J. M. Singer & Co's Sewing Machine Manufactory.

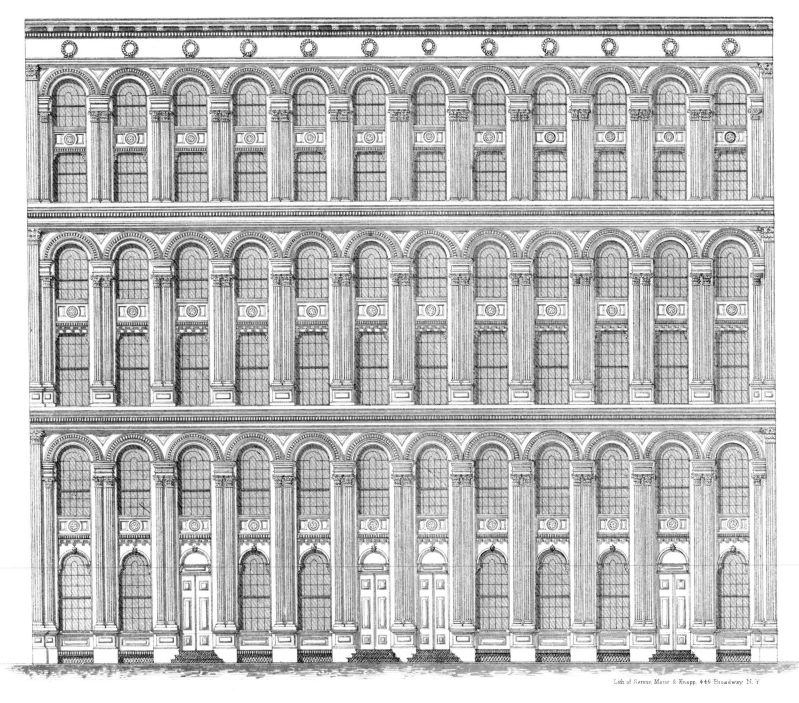

ARCHITECTURAL IRON WORKS, NEW YORK.

Lith of Sarony, Major & Knapp. 449 Broadway N. Y.

Scale_ one inch to twelve feet.

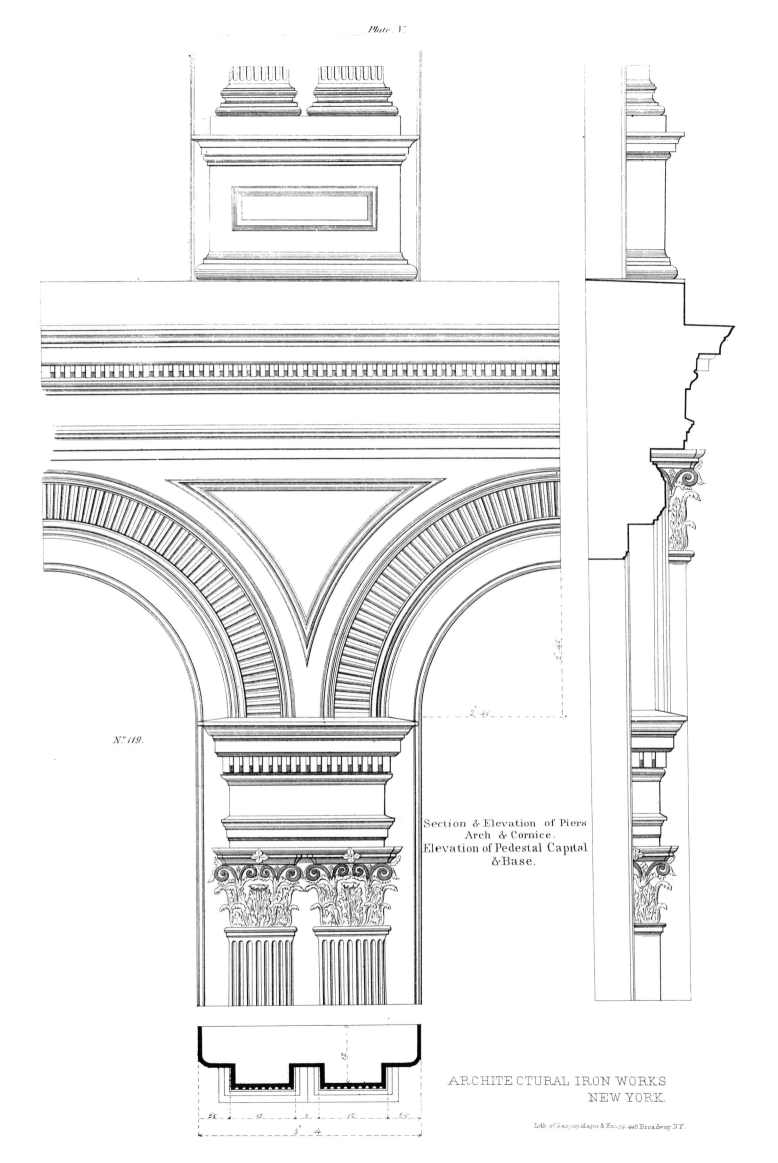

Plate V.

Nº 119.

Section & Elevation of Piers
Arch & Cornice.
Elevation of Pedestal Capital
& Base.

ARCHITECTURAL IRON WORKS
NEW YORK.

Lith of Sarony Major & Knapp 449 Broadway N.Y.

Plate VI.

Section of Singer Building.

N.º 16

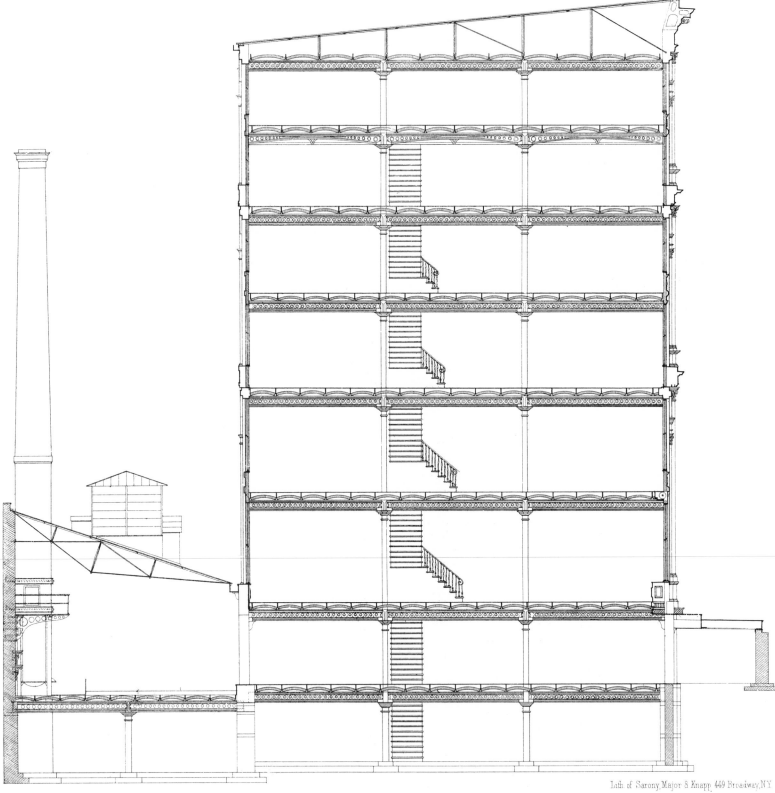

ARCHITECTURAL IRON WORKS,—NEW-YORK

Plate VII.

No. 1.

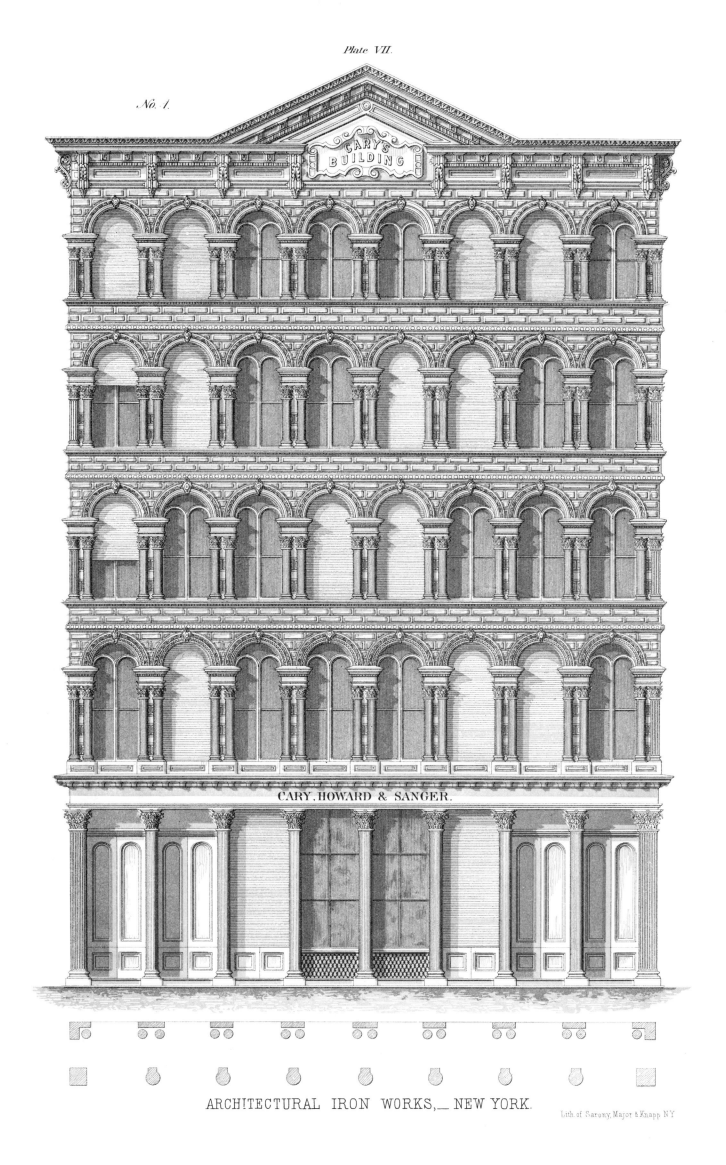

CARY'S BUILDING

CARY, HOWARD & SANGER.

ARCHITECTURAL IRON WORKS,__ NEW YORK.

Lith. of Sarony, Major & Knapp, N.Y

Plate. VIII.

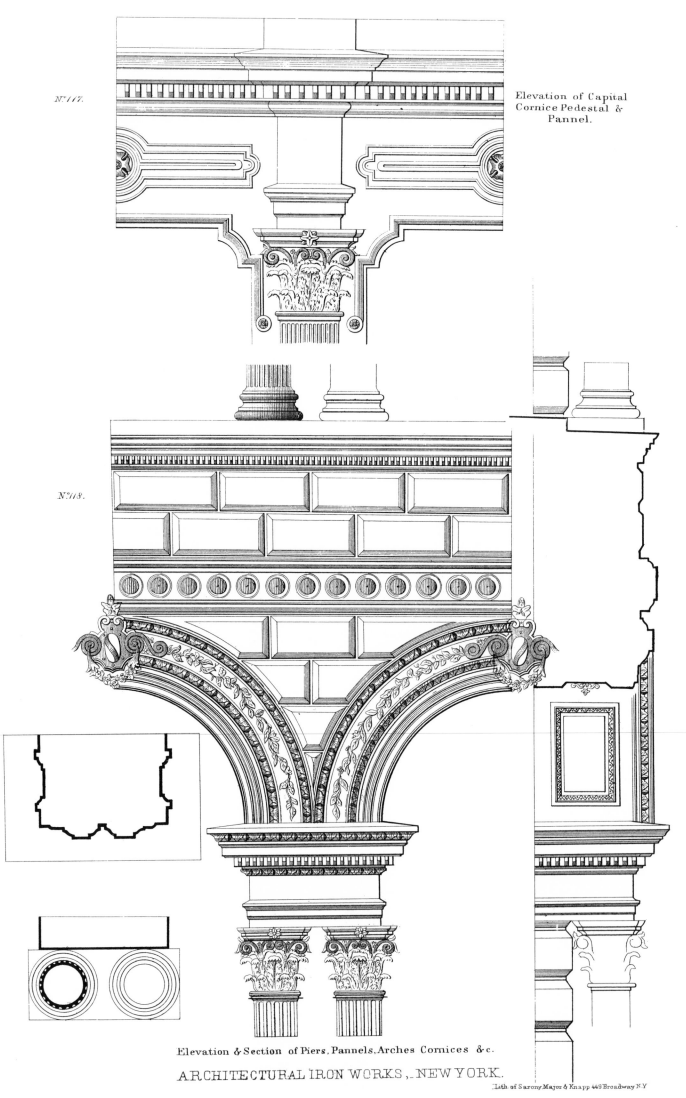

Nº 117.

Elevation of Capital
Cornice Pedestal &
Pannel.

Nº 118.

Elevation & Section of Piers, Pannels, Arches Cornices &c.

ARCHITECTURAL IRON WORKS, NEW YORK.

Lith. of Sarony, Major & Knapp 449 Broadway N.Y.

Plate IX.

No: 29.

ARCHITECTURAL IRON WORKS, — NEW-YORK.

Lith of Sarony, Major & Knapp, 449 Broadway, N.Y.

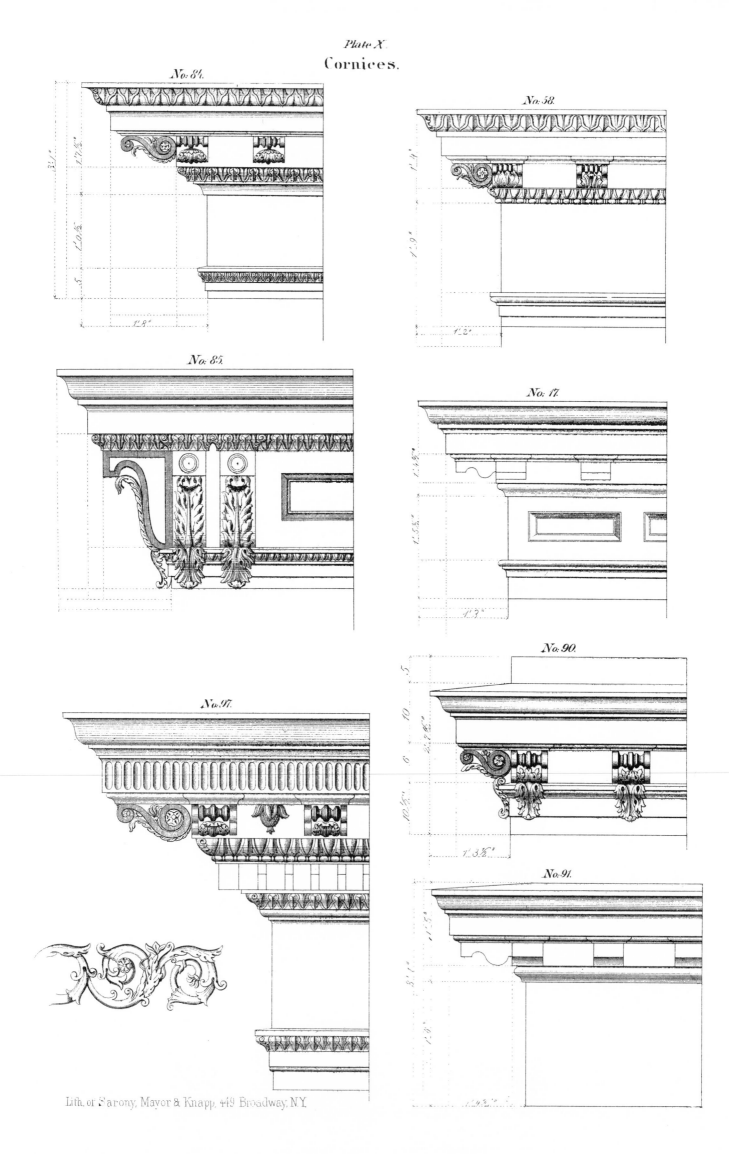

Plate X.

Cornices.

No: 84.

No: 58.

No: 85.

No: 17.

No: 97.

No: 90.

No: 91.

Plate XI.

OFFICE OF

GROVER & BAKER S.M.C?

Grover & Baker

3' 0"

8' 0"

1' 10"

13' 6"

1' 6"

14' 6"

1' 6"

15' 6"

Total height 58' 6"

Lith of Sarony Major & Knapp, 449 Broadway N.Y.

ARCHITECTURAL IRON WORKS,— NEW-YORK.

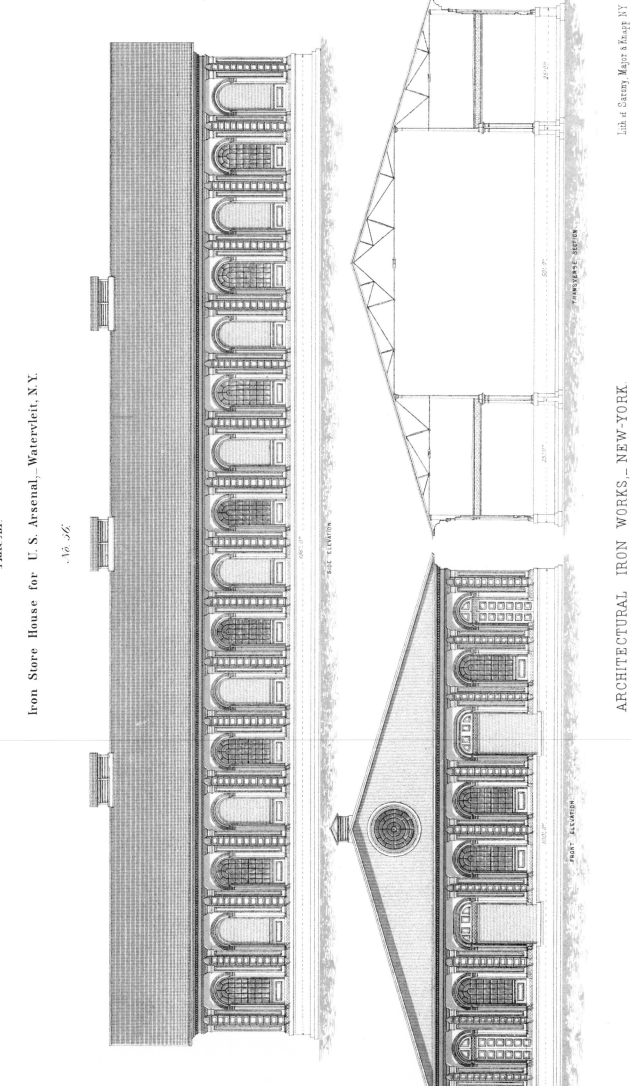

Plate XII.

Iron Store House for U. S. Arsenal,— Watervleit, N.Y.

No. 56.

SIDE ELEVATION.

TRANSVERSE SECTION.

FRONT ELEVATION.

ARCHITECTURAL IRON WORKS,— NEW-YORK.

Lith of Sarony, Major & Knapp N.Y.

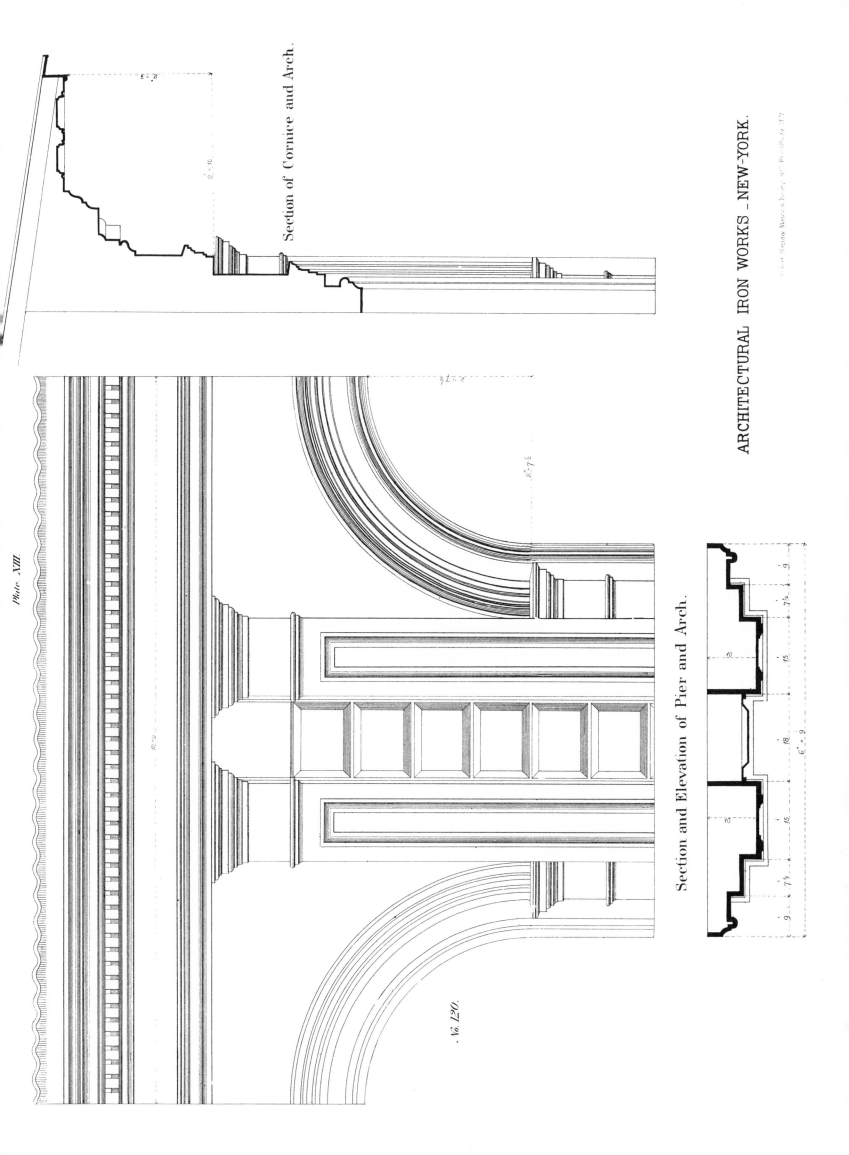

Plate. XIII.

Section of Cornice and Arch.

No. 120.

Section and Elevation of Pier and Arch.

ARCHITECTURAL IRON WORKS - NEW-YORK.

ARCHITECTURAL IRON WORKS,—NEW-YORK.

Plate XV

Designs for Store Fronts.

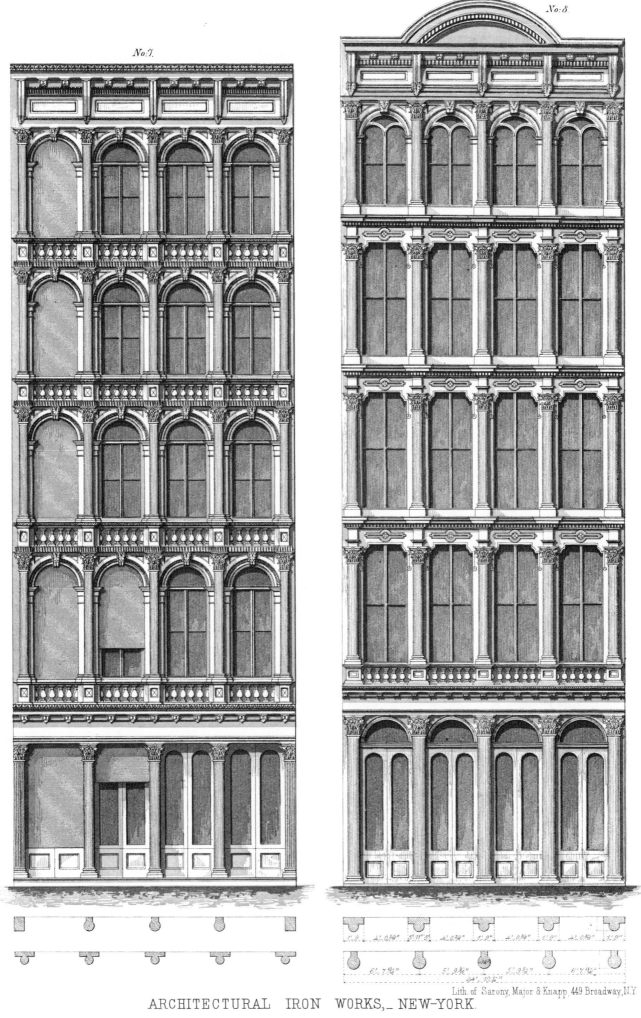

No: 7.

No: 8.

Lith. of Sarony, Major & Knapp, 449 Broadway, N.Y.

ARCHITECTURAL IRON WORKS,_ NEW-YORK.

Plate XVI

Cornices Balustrades and Pedestals.

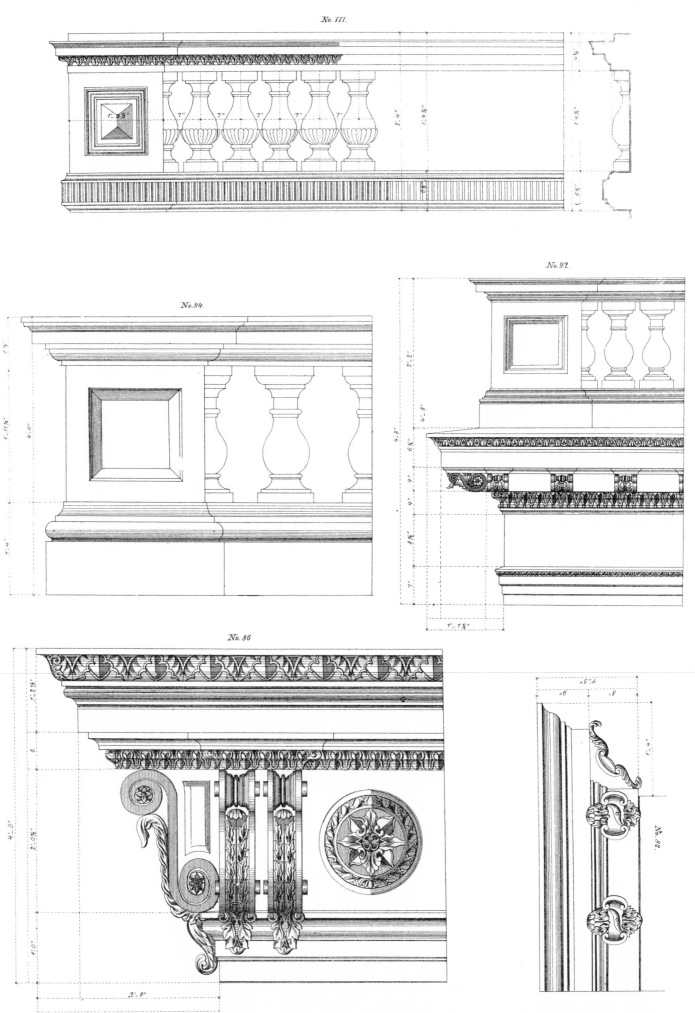

No. 111.

No. 94.

No. 92.

No. 86.

Lith of Sarony Major & Knapp 449 Broadway NY.

ARCHITECTURAL IRON WORKS NEW YORK

Plate XVII

Designs for Store Fronts.

No. 5.

No. 6.

Lith of Sarony Major & Knapp. 449 Broadway, N.Y

ARCHITECTURAL IRON WORKS,— NEW-YORK.

Plate XVIII.

Cornices.

N.º 100.

N.º 103.

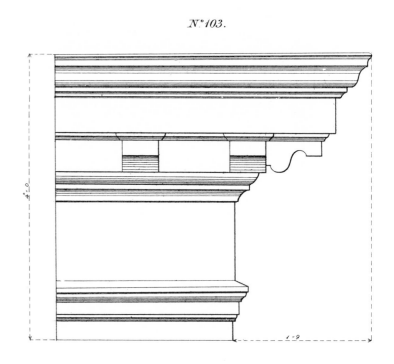

N.º 101.

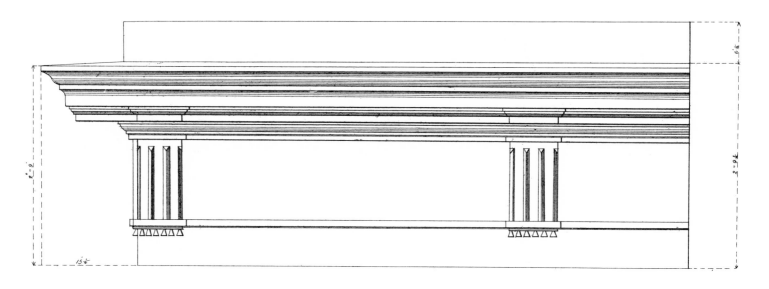

N.º 102.

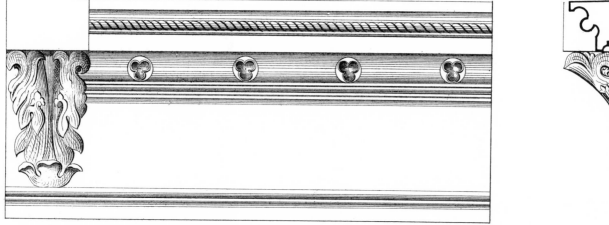

ARCHITECTURAL IRON WORKS, NEW YORK.

Lith. of Sarony, Major & Knapp 449 Broadway N.Y.

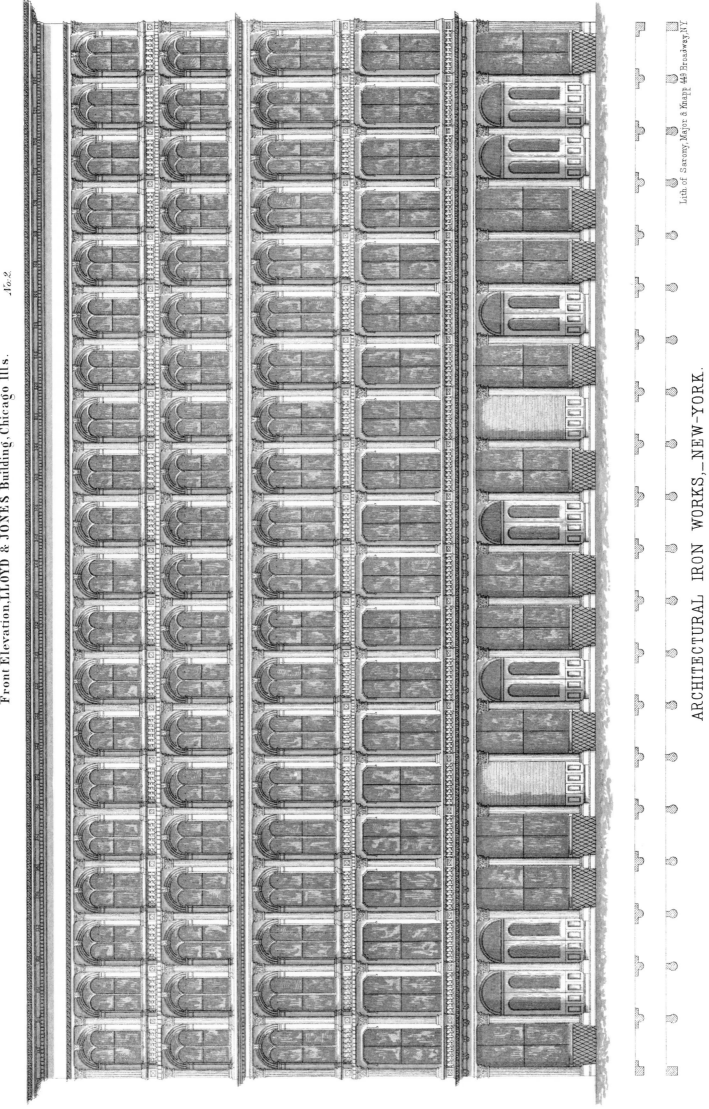

Plate XIX.   No. 2.

Front Elevation, LLOYD & JONES Building, Chicago Ills.

ARCHITECTURAL IRON WORKS,—NEW-YORK.

Lith. of Sarony, Major & Knapp 449 Broadway, NY

Plate. XX.

Cornices.

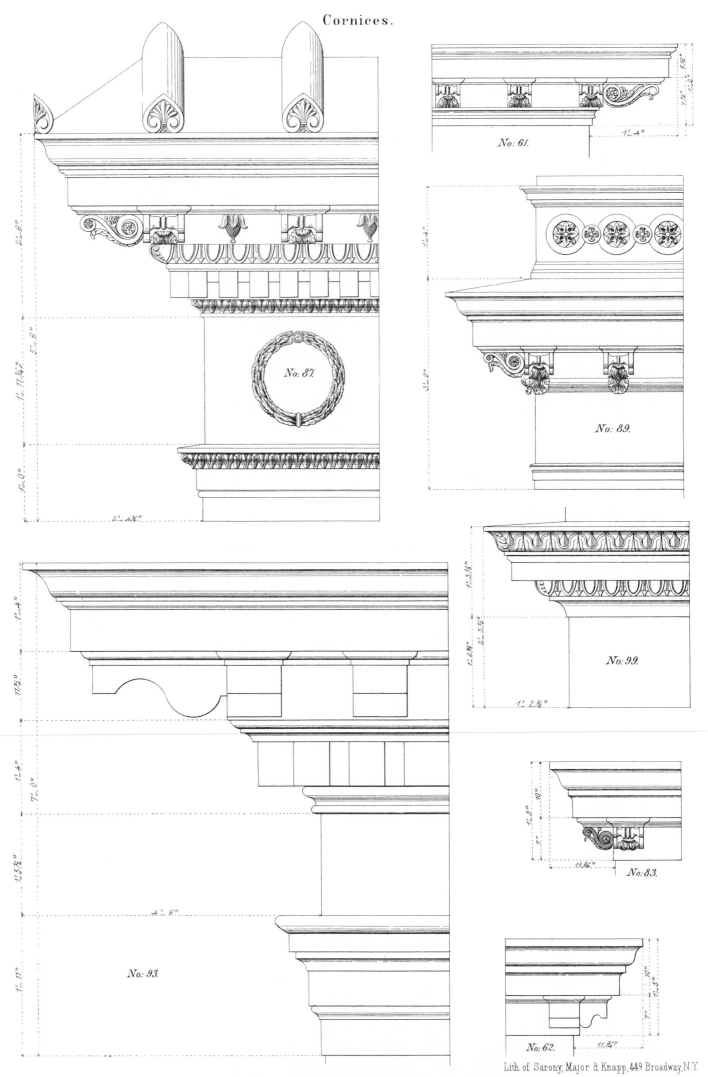

No: 61.

No: 87.

No: 89.

No: 99.

No: 93.

No: 83.

No: 62.

Lith. of Sarony, Major & Knapp, 449 Broadway, N.Y.

ARCHITECTURAL IRON WORKS, — NEW-YORK.

Plate XXI.

Design for Store Front.

No: 37.

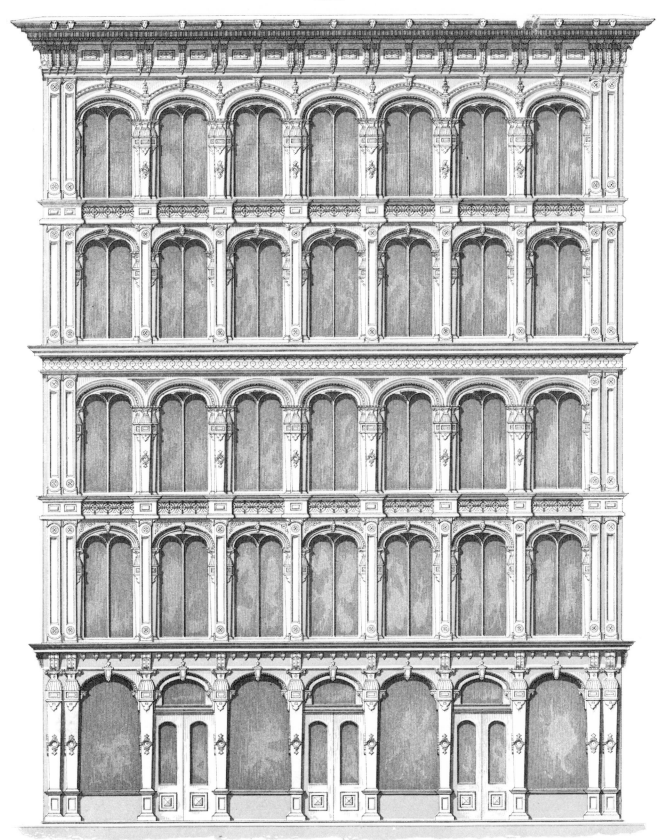

Lith. of Sarony, Major & Knapp, 449 Broadway, N.Y.

ARCHITECTURAL IRON WORKS,— NEW-YORK.

Plate XXII.

Nᵒ 58

Store Front 130 Broadway.

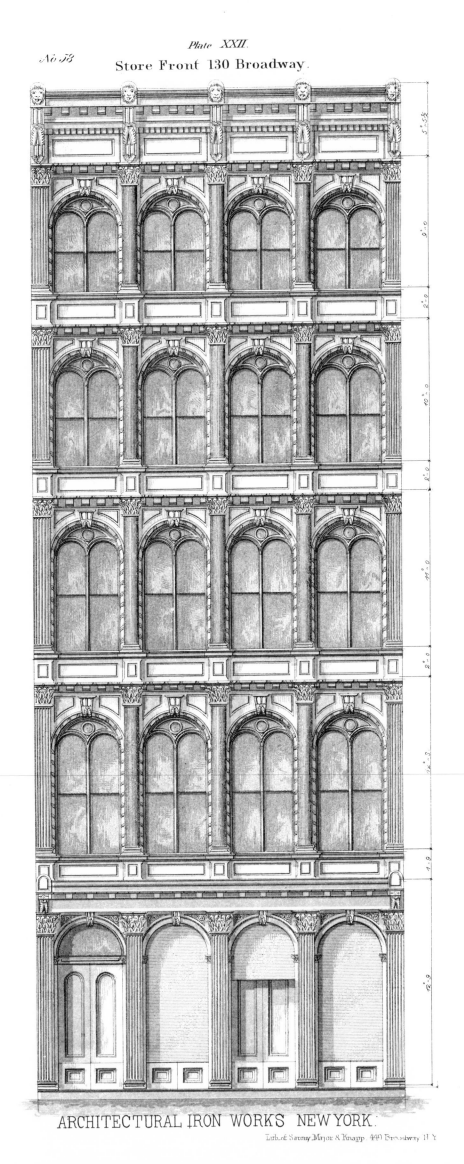

ARCHITECTURAL IRON WORKS NEW YORK.

Lith. of Sarony, Major & Knapp. 449 Broadway N.Y.

Plate XXIII.

Cornices.

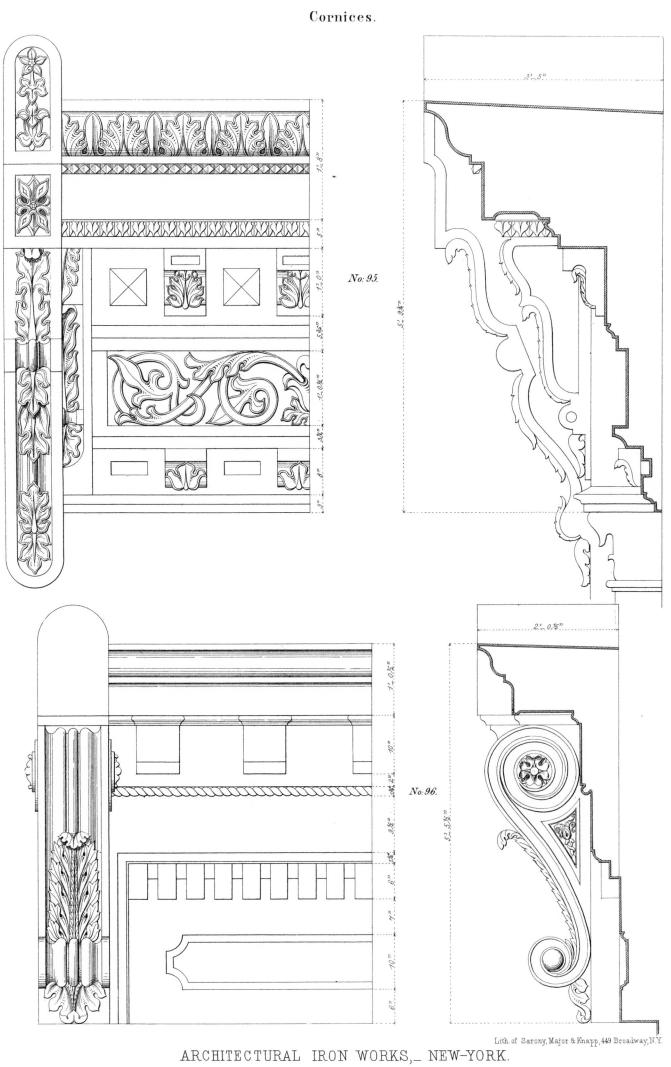

No: 95.

No: 96.

ARCHITECTURAL IRON WORKS,— NEW-YORK.

Plate XXIV.

Front Elevation of first Story

No:63.

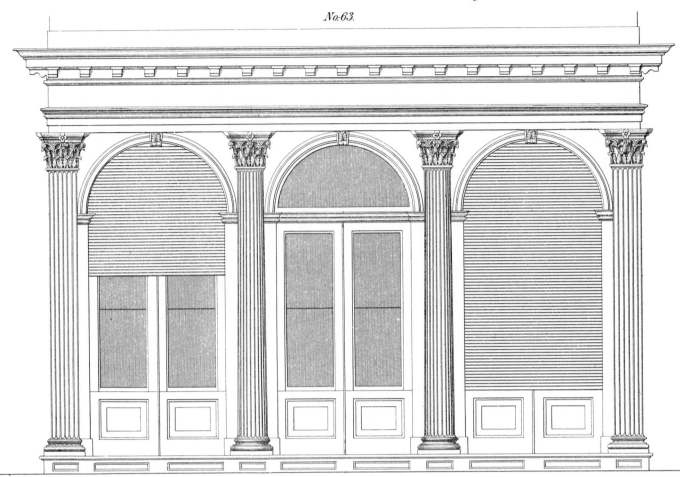

No: 64.

Lith of Sarony, Major & Knapp, 449 Broadway, N.Y.

ARCHITECTURAL IRON WORKS, — NEW-YORK

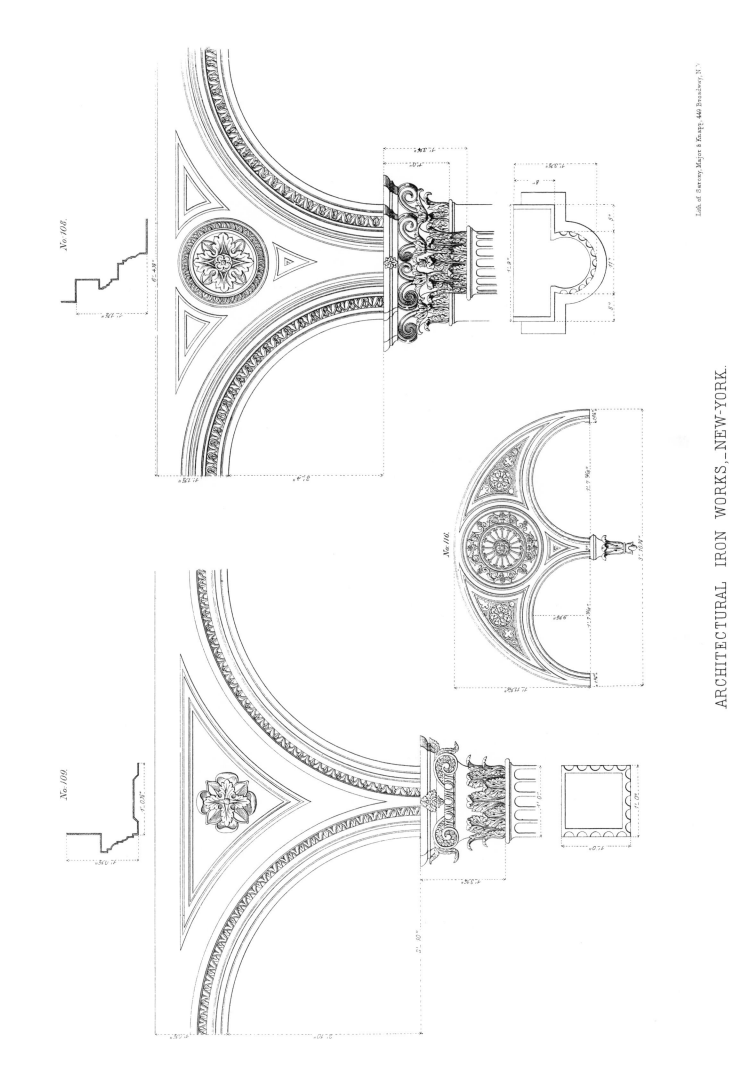

Plate XVI

Arches and Tracery. Capitals with Section of Piers.

No. 108.

No. 109.

No. 116.

ARCHITECTURAL IRON WORKS,—NEW-YORK.

Lith of Sarony, Major & Knapp, 449 Broadway, N.Y.

Iron Front for
Mr John McCregor.
Newark N.J.

Plate XXVI.

No:60.

J. M^cCREGOR.

ARCHITECTURAL IRON WORKS,__NEW—YORK.

Scale one Inch to Eight feet.

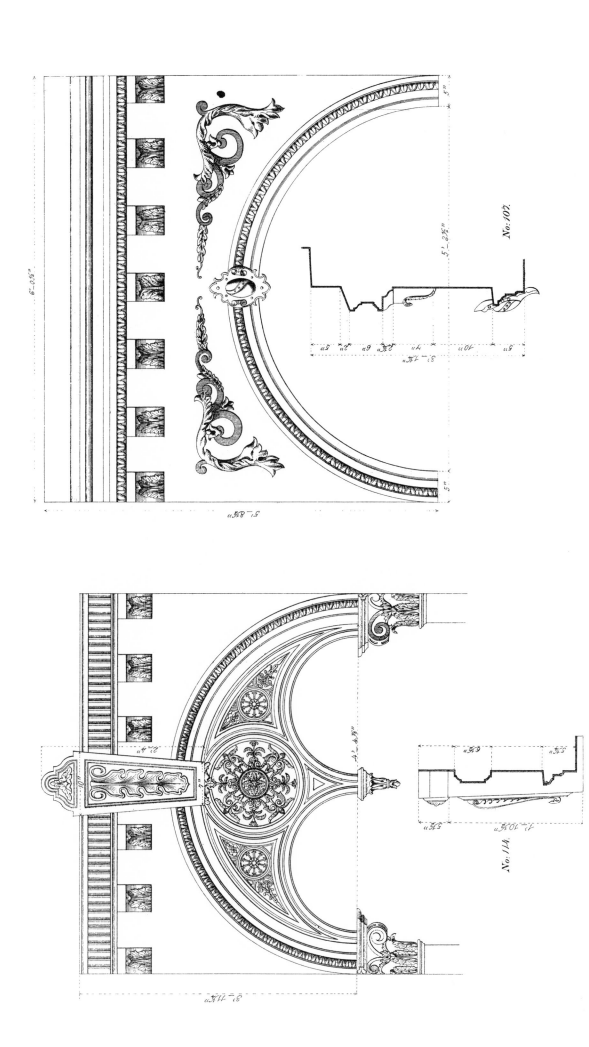

Plate XXVII

Arches, Keys, and Arch Ornaments.

No. 107.

No. 114.

ARCHITECTURAL IRON WORKS,—NEW-YORK.

Lith. of Sarony Major & Knapp, 449 Broadway, N.Y.

Plate XXVIII.

Designs for Store Fronts.

No. 62.

No. 66.

SOLOMON & HART.

No. 65.

R. NICHOLLS, PETERBORO. C.W.

ARCHITECTURAL IRON WORKS,—NEW-YORK.

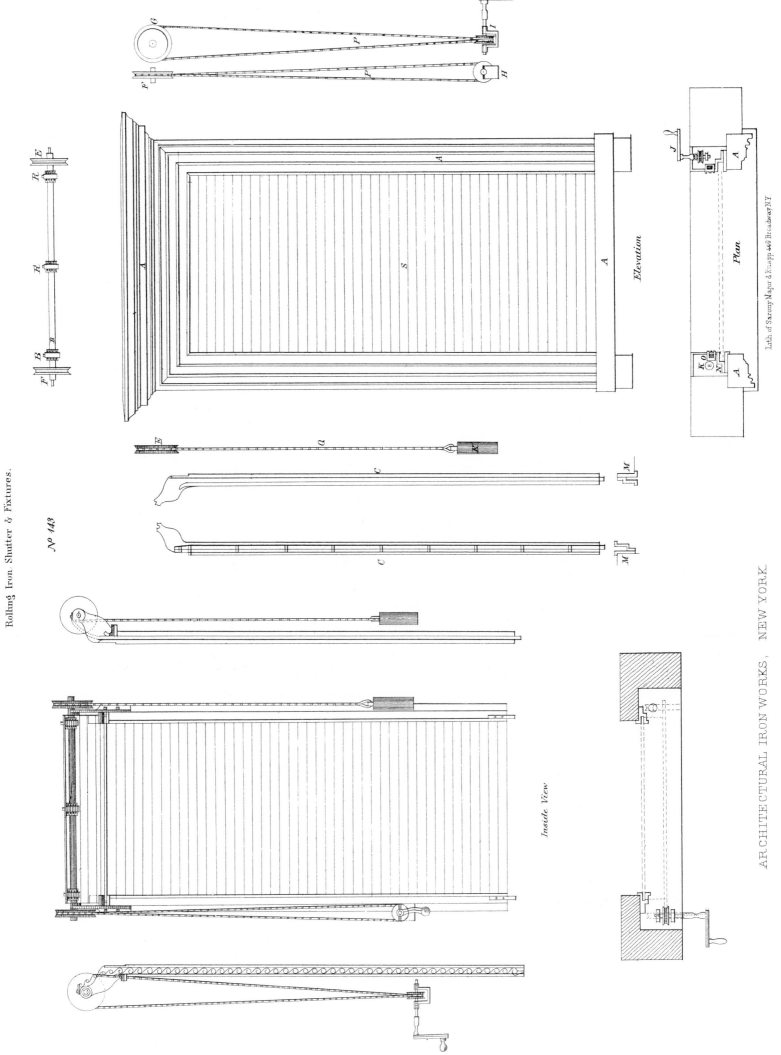

Plate. XXIX.

Rolling Iron Shutter & Fixtures.

Nº 143

Elevation

Plan

Inside View

ARCHITECTURAL IRON WORKS, NEW YORK

Lith of Sarony Major & Knapp 449 Broadway NY

Plate XXX.

Nº 21.

ODD FELLOWS HALL.

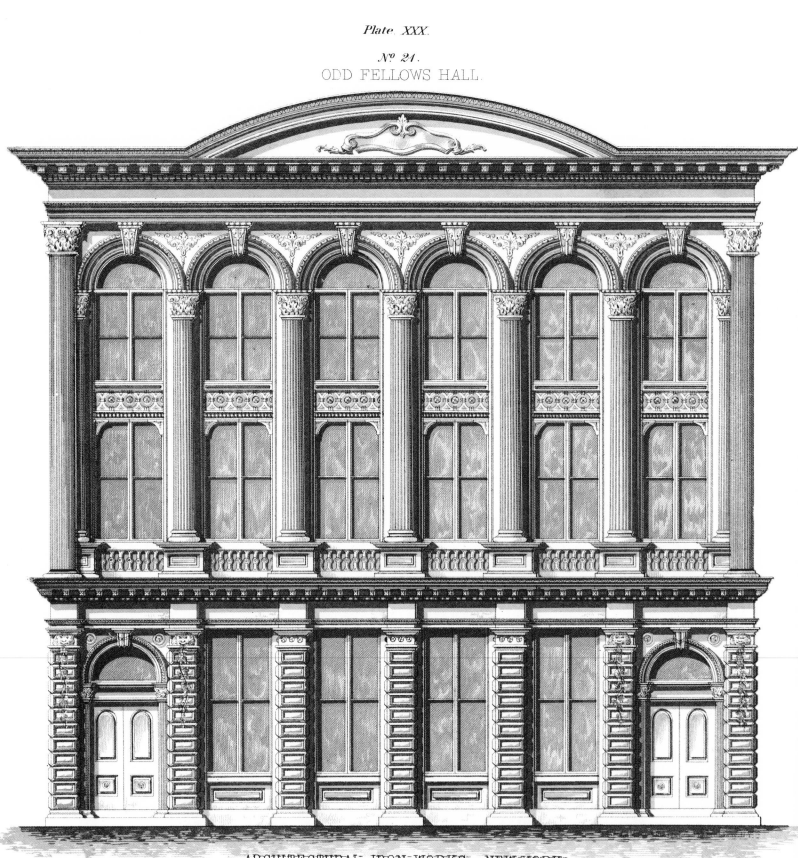

ARCHITECTURAL IRON WORKS, — NEW-YORK.

Plate XXXI

Elevations of 1st Story Fronts.

N.º 50.

N.º 51.

N.º 52.

N.º 53.

N.º 54.

N.º 55.

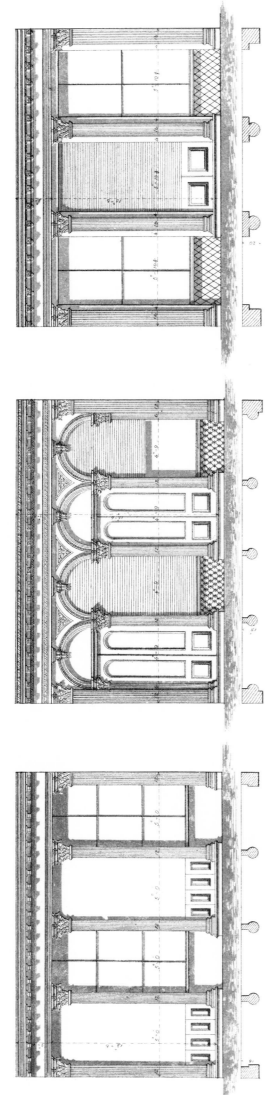
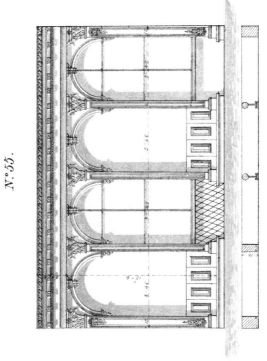
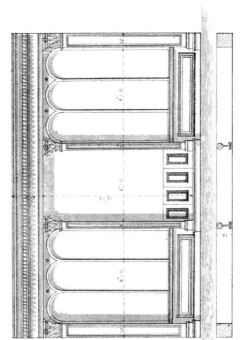
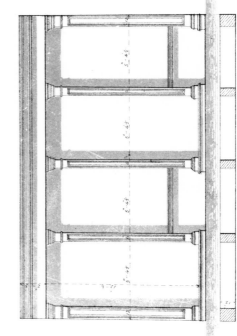

Lith. of Sarony Major & Knapp 449 Broadway N.Y.

ARCHITECTURAL IRON WORKS, NEW YORK

Plate XXXII.

Cornices Arches & Arches Ornamental.

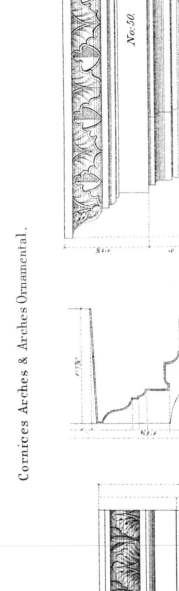

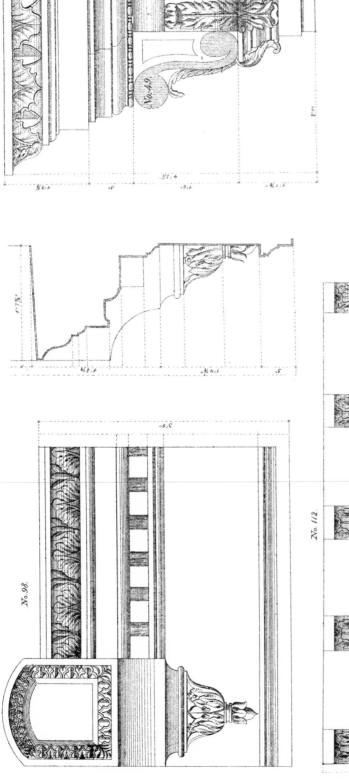

No: 50.

No: 51.

No. 92.

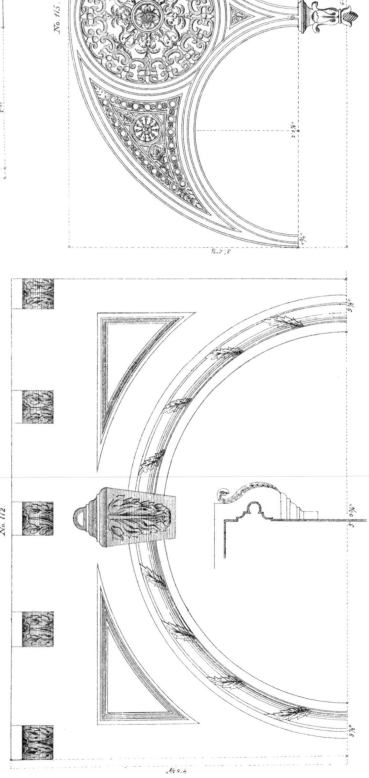

No: 115.

No: 112.

Lith of Sarony Major & Knapp, 449 Broadway, N.Y.

ARCHITECTURAL IRON WORKS NEW YORK.

Plate XXXIII.

Iron Store Front for W.B Greenlaw & Co.
Memphis   Tenn.

No. 69.

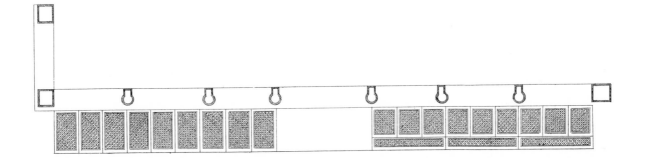

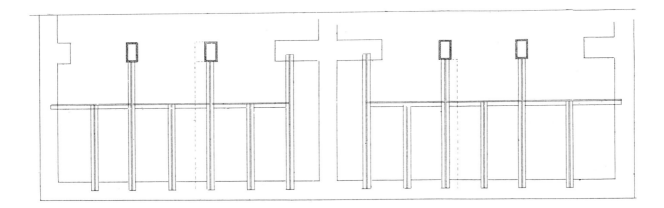

ARCHITECTURAL IRON WORKS.— NEW-YORK

Lith. of Sarony Major & Knapp 449 Broadway N.Y.

Plate XXXIV.

No: 31.

No: 32.

ARCHITECTURAL IRON WORKS, __ NEW-YORK.

Plate XXXV.

No:33.

No:34.

ARCHITECTURAL IRON WORKS,—NEW-YORK.

Plate XXXVI.

Designs for Store Fronts

No. 48.

No. 46.

No. 42.

ARCHITECTURAL IRON WORKS.– NEW-YORK.

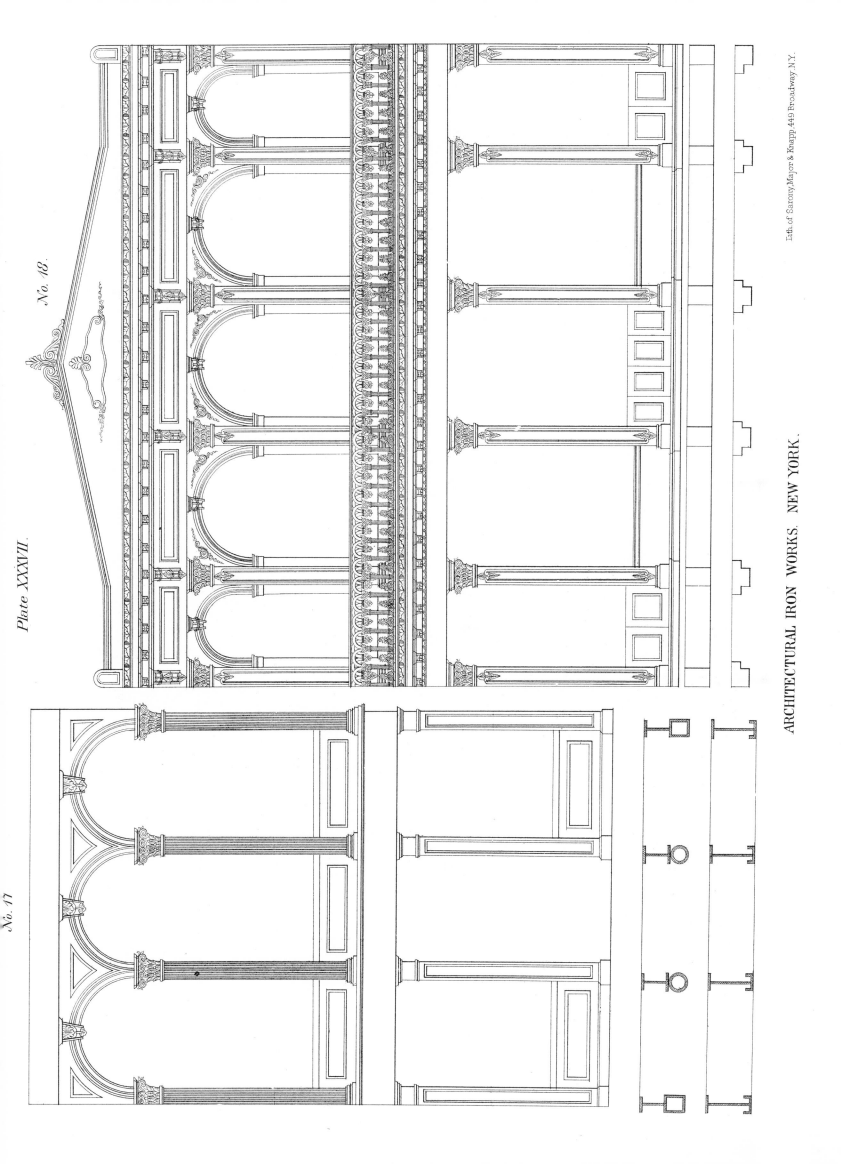

Plate XXXVII.

No. 18.

No. 17.

ARCHITECTURAL IRON WORKS. NEW YORK.

Lith. of Sarony, Major & Knapp, 449 Broadway, N.Y.

Plate XXXVIII.

ARCHITECTURAL IRON WORKS,— NEW-YORK.

Plate. XXXIX.

Arches, Keys, Capitals & Section of Piers.

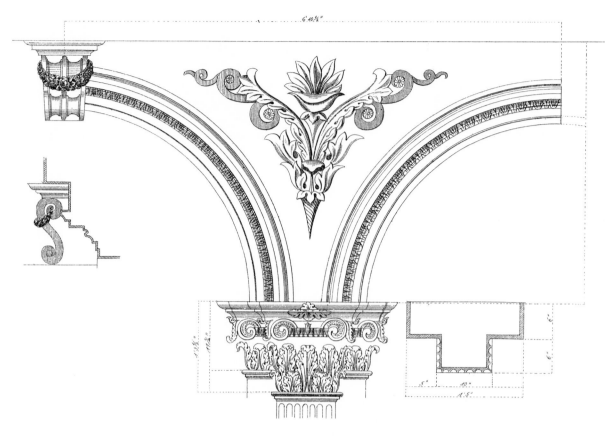

No. 106.

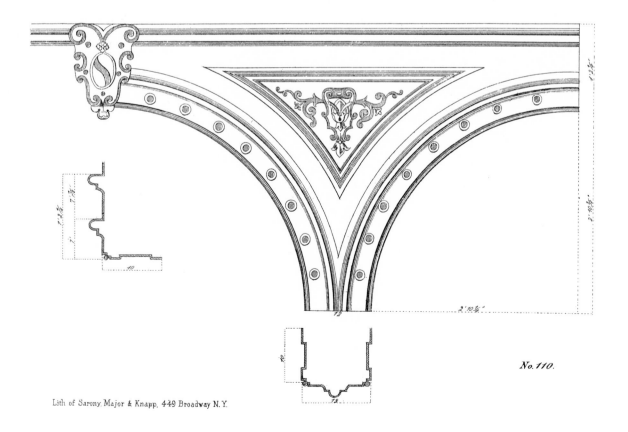

Lith of Sarony, Major & Knapp, 449 Broadway N.Y.

No. 110.

ARCHITECTURAL IRON WORKS, NEW YORK.

Plate XL.

Store Front for Mr. Kramer
Boston, Mass   No:67.

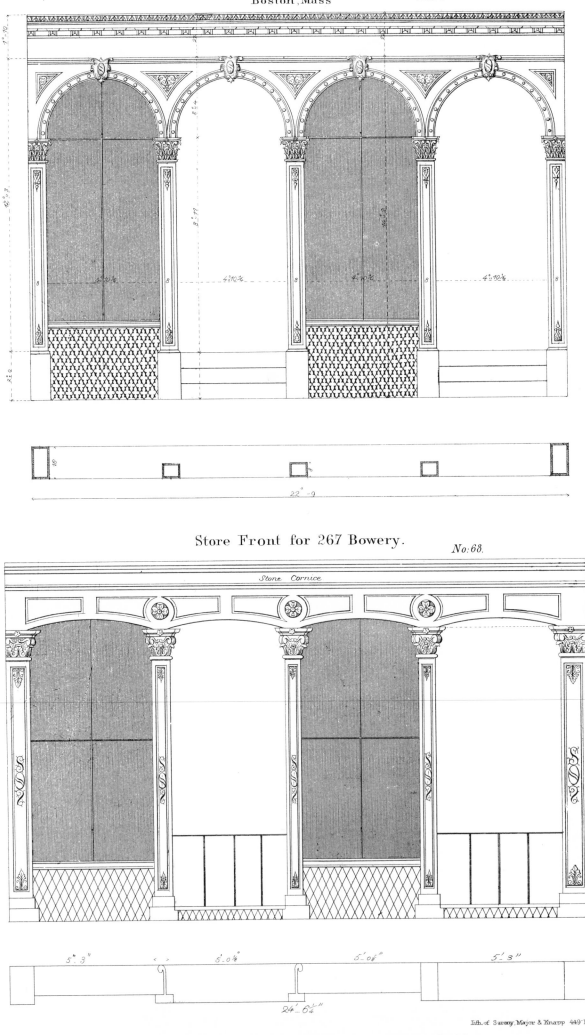

Store Front for 267 Bowery.
No:68.

Stone Cornice

Lith. of Sarony, Major & Knapp 449 Broadway N.Y.

ARCHITECTURAL IRON WORKS.___NEW YORK

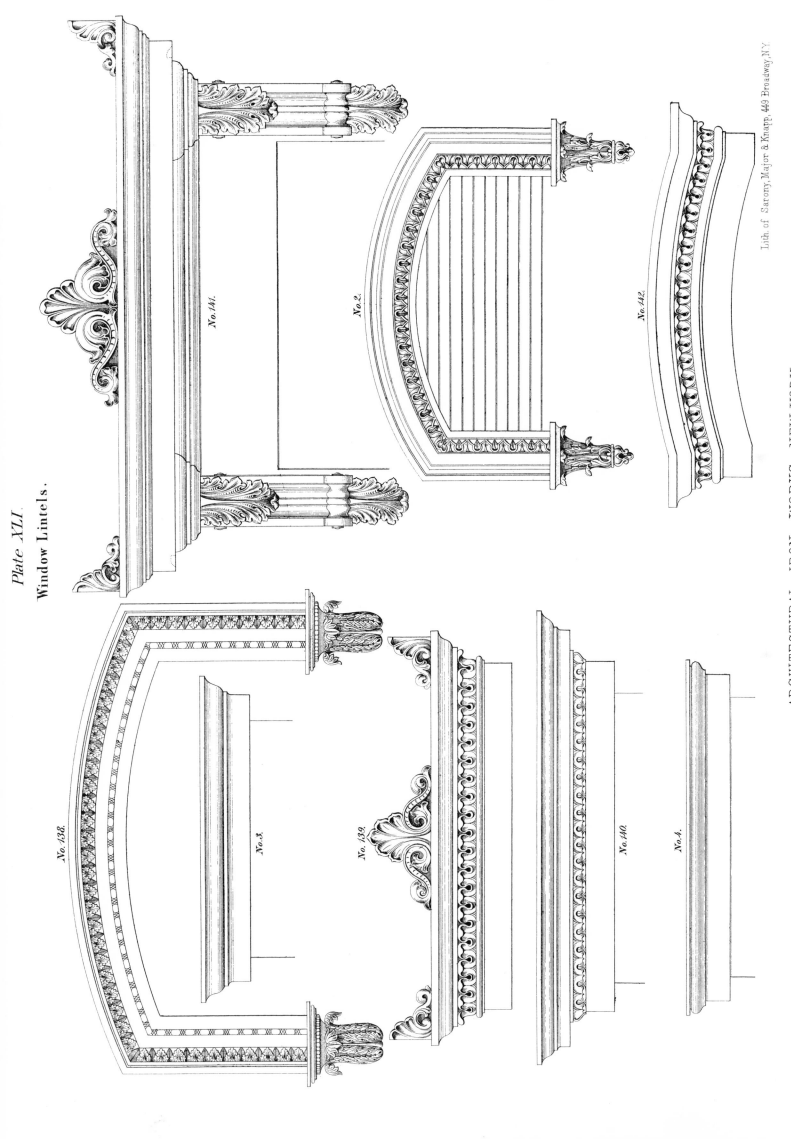

Plate XLI.
Window Lintels.

No. 141.

No. 2.

No. 142.

No. 138.

No. 3.

No. 139.

No. 140.

No. 4.

Lith. of Sarony, Major & Knapp, 449 Broadway, N.Y.

ARCHITECTURAL IRON WORKS,—NEW-YORK.

Plate XLII.

Window Lintels.

No. 5.A

No. 68.

No. 73.

No. 5. B

No. 121

No. 122

No. 70.

No. 125.

No. 123.

No. 124

No 77

Lith of Sarony Major & Knapp, 449 Broadway

ARCHITECTURAL IRON WORKS NEW YORK.

Plate XLIII.

Awning Posts & Rod.

1

1

Window Lintel Architraves & Sill.

ARCHITECTURAL IRON WORKS,_NEW-YORK.

Lith. of Sarony, Major & Knapp, 449 B'way, N.Y.

Plate XLIV

Window Lintels. Lamp Post, etc.

No.: 145.

7'0"

No.: 144.

7'0"

32"

No.: 126

38"

No.: 128.

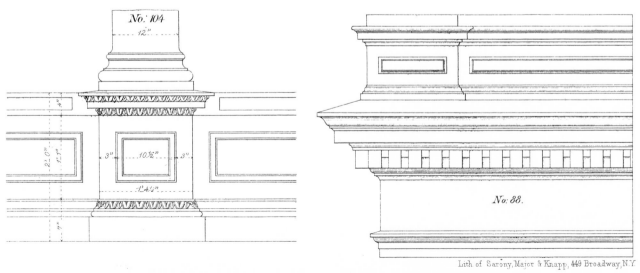

No.: 104

12"

No.: 88.

ARCHITECTURAL IRON WORKS,_ NEW-YORK

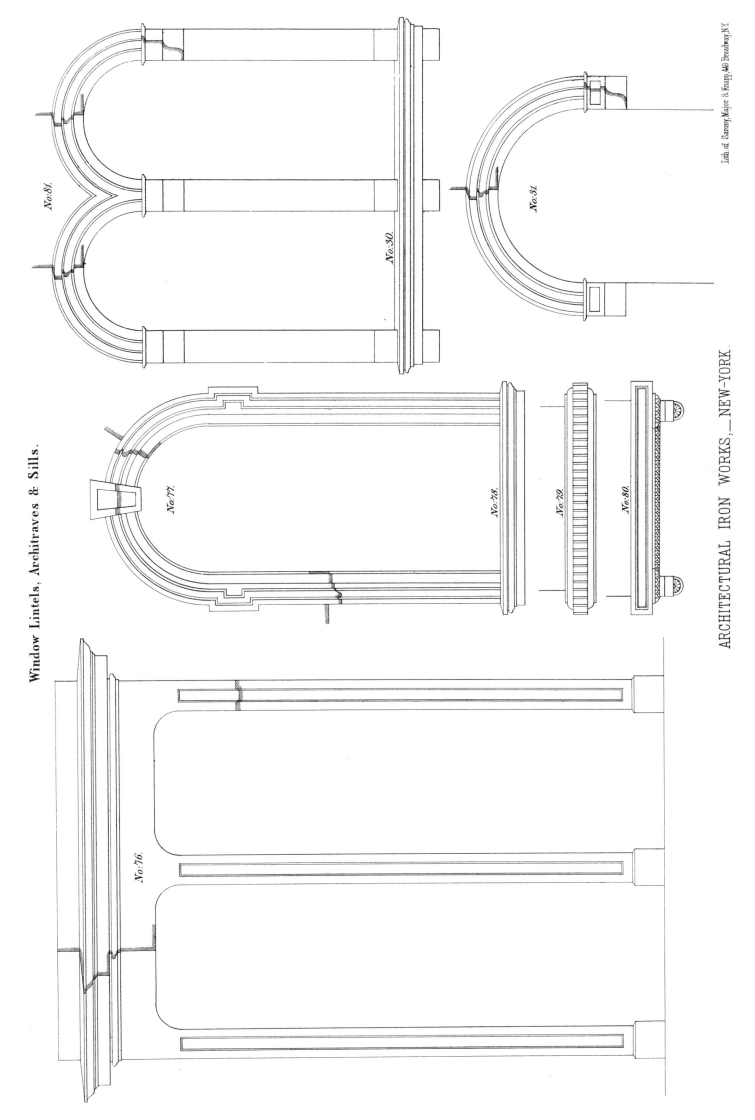

Plate XLV.

Window Lintels, Architraves & Sills.

No: 81.

No: 30.

No: 31.

No: 77.

No: 78.

No: 79.

No: 80.

No: 76.

ARCHITECTURAL IRON WORKS,—NEW-YORK.

Lith. of Sarony, Major & Knapp, 449 Broadway, N.Y.

Plate XLVI.

No.20

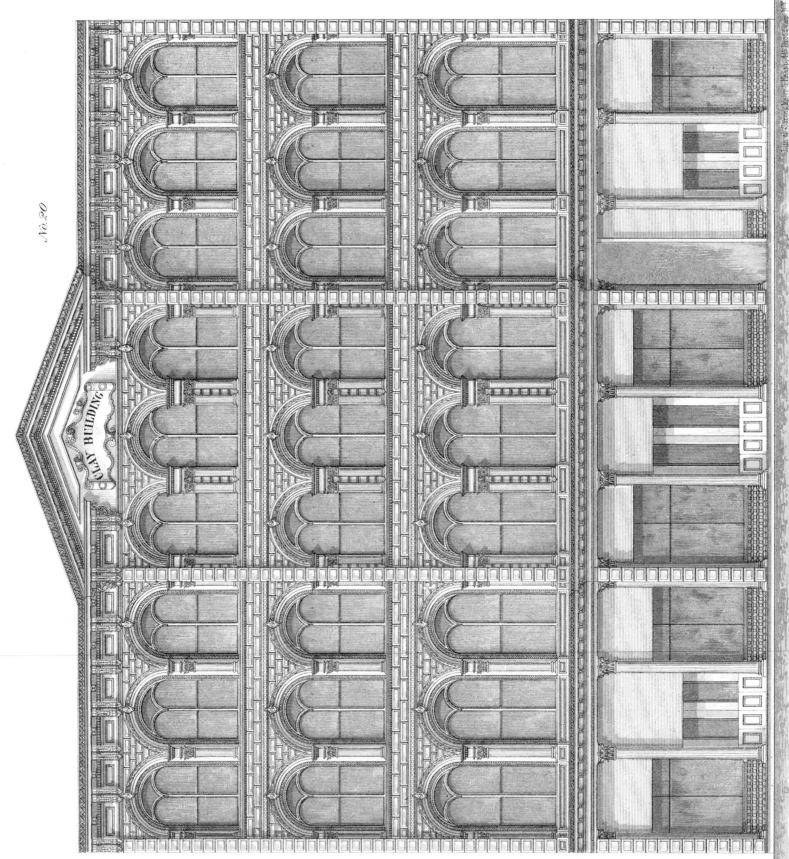

CLAY BUILDING

ARCHITECTURAL IRON WORKS, NEW YORK.

Plate XLVII.

Consoles and Brackets

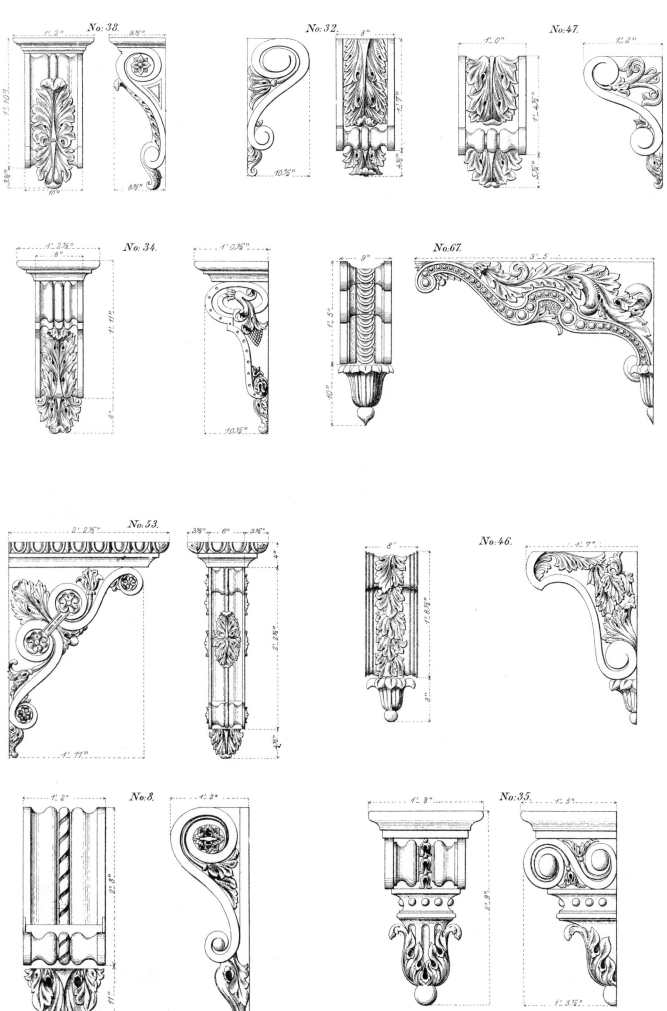

ARCHITECTURAL IRON WORKS, — NEW-YORK

Plate XLVIII.

Consoles Corbels & Urn.

No.275

No.277

No: 278

No.279

No.7.

No.276

No.280

No. 281
4 inch.

No. 282
8"

No.28.

No. 6.

No. 283
8 inch.

No. 284.
6 inch.

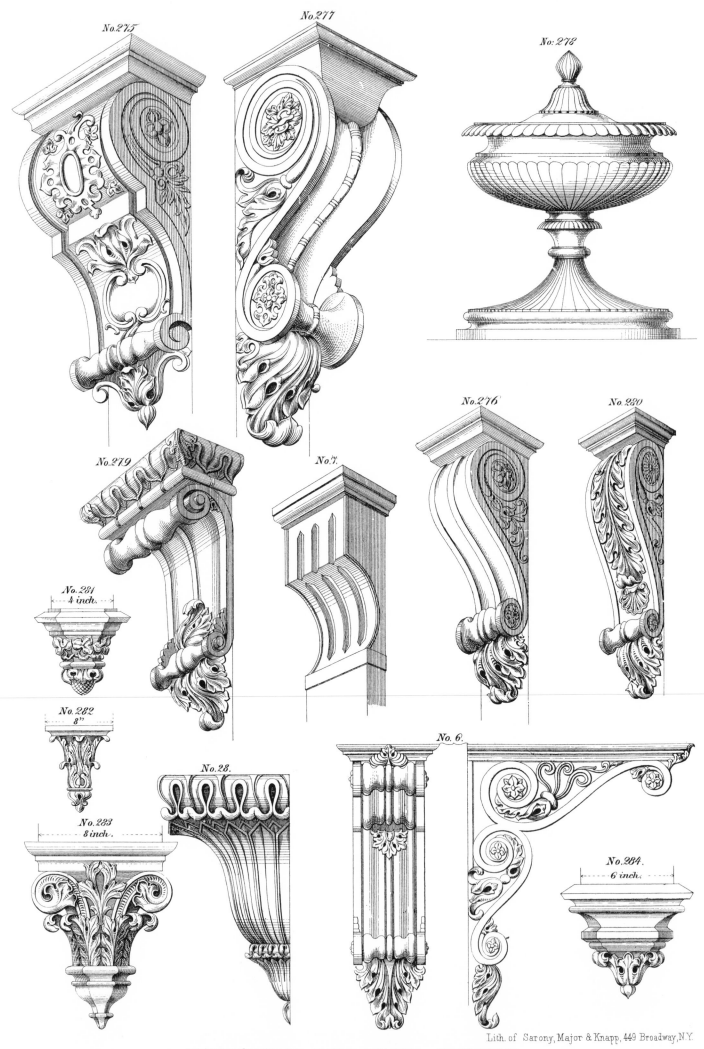

ARCHITECTURAL IRON WORKS, NEW-YORK.

Plate XLIX.

Elevations and Sections of Columns and Capitals.

ARCHITECTURAL IRON WORKS,—NEW-YORK.

Gothic Capital.

Stewart Capital.

Stewart Capital.

Plate. L.

No. 148

No 147

No 146

Lith. of Sarony Major & Knapp, 449 Broadway, N.Y.

ARCHITECTURAL IRON WORKS,— NEW-YORK.

No:159.

No:161.

No:160.

Corinthian Order.

Composite Order.

Ionic Order.

Doric Order.

Tuscan Order.

Lith. of Sarony, Major & Knapp, 449 Broadway N.Y.

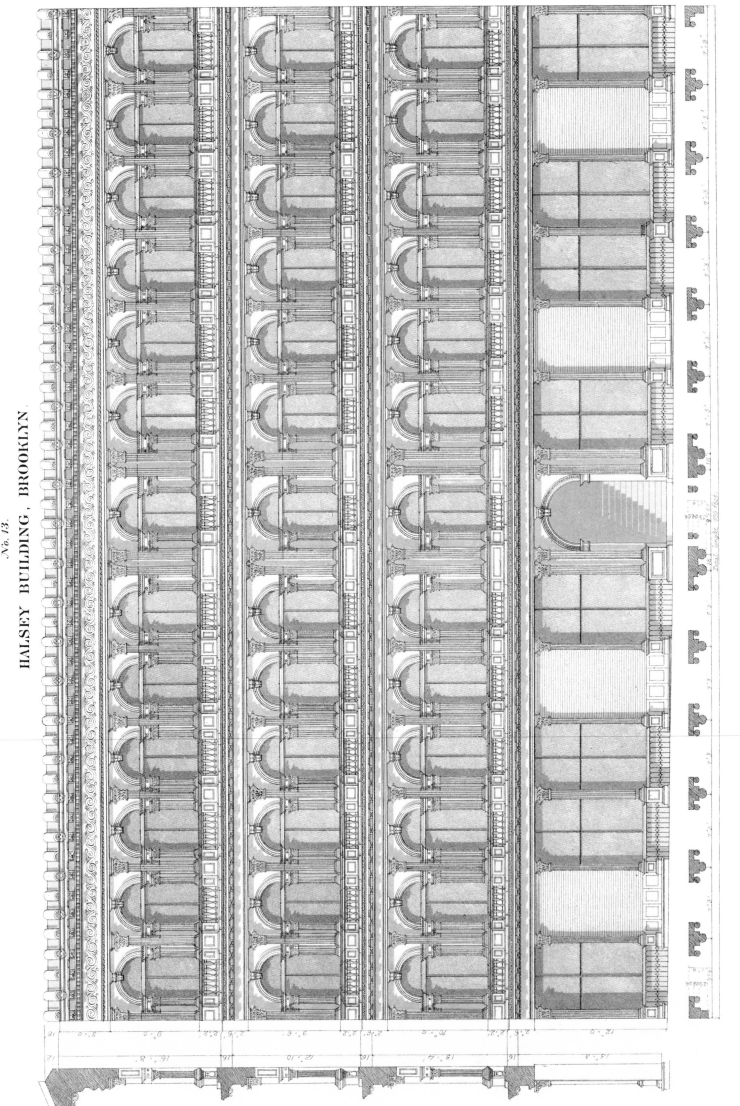

Plate LII.
No. 13.

HALSEY BUILDING, BROOKLYN.

Lith. of Sarony Major & Knapp. 449 Broadway. N.Y.

ARCHITECTURAL IRON WORKS – NEW YORK.

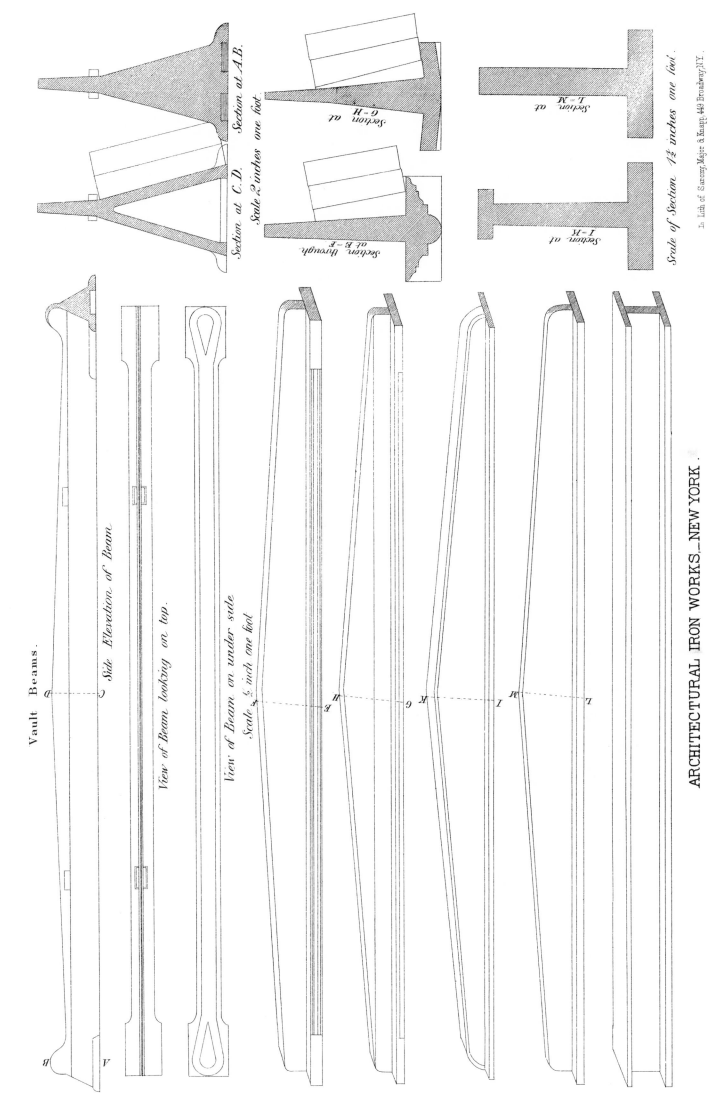

Plate LIII.

Vault Beams.

Side Elevation of Beam.

View of Beam looking on top.

View of Beam on under side.

Scale ⅓ inch one foot.

Section at A.B.

Section at C.D.

Scale 2 inches one foot.

Section at G–H.

Section through at E–F.

Section at L–M.

Section at I–K.

Scale of Section 1½ inches one foot.

In Lith. of Sarony, Major & Knapp, 449 Broadway, N.Y.

ARCHITECTURAL IRON WORKS.—NEW YORK.

Plate LIV.

No 3.

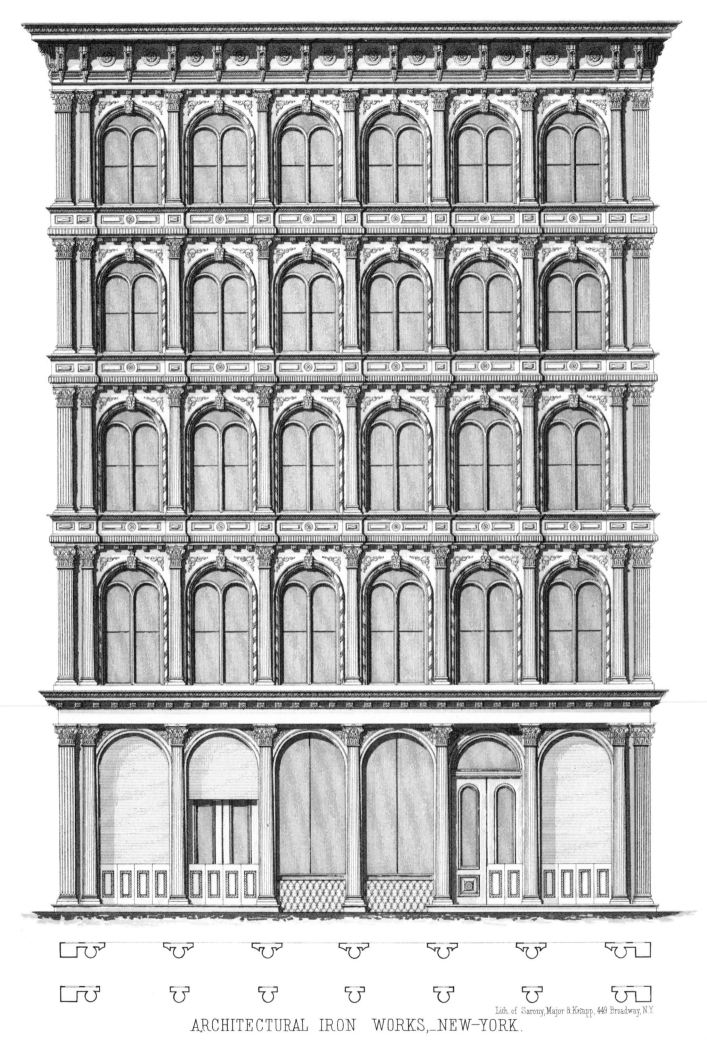

Lith. of Sarony, Major & Knapp, 449 Broadway, N.Y.

ARCHITECTURAL IRON WORKS,—NEW-YORK.

Plate LV.

Design for Front of Dwelling House.

No 41

ARCHITECTURAL IRON WORKS,—NEW-YORK.

PATENT METALLIC WINDOW BLINDS
BURGLAR & FIRE-PROOF.

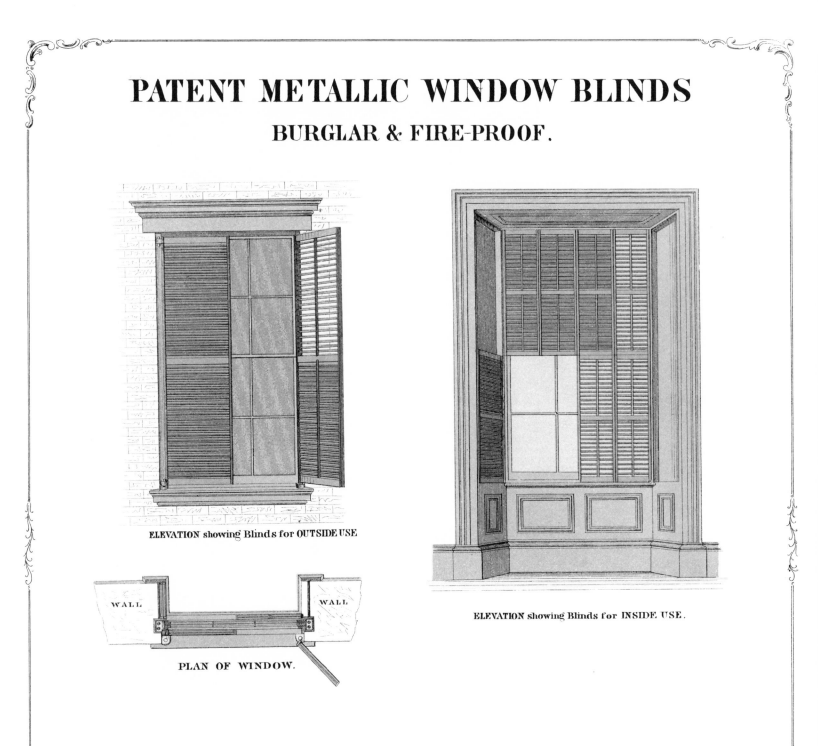

ELEVATION showing Blinds for OUTSIDE USE

PLAN OF WINDOW.

ELEVATION showing Blinds for INSIDE USE.

    This Blind obviates all the difficulties and inconveniences of the wooden Blind, and is designed to supersede the folding iron shutter and the outside and inside wooden blind and shutter. It is fire-proof and by actual experiment is shown to resist the fire much longer than the ordinary iron shutter, and water thrown on it while hot will not curve, warp or open it so as to expose the window to the flames. This Blind does not shrink, warp or settle by exposure to solar or artificial heat or by atmospheric changes, thus freeing it from those objections to the wooden blind, which so try the patience of House-keepers. The wires are always in order and can not be pulled out, the slats remain unbroken and can be so adjusted as to let in the exact amount of light and air required. It is self-fastening and fastenings are always in order. It is substantial and, unlike the wooden blind, requires little or no repairs and is capable of the highest finish and ornament. The inside blinds are specially adapted to first class dwellings, churches &c.

    Many of the first Architects and Builders of this and other Cities have given these Blinds their unqualified approval. They have been adopted by various banking houses and dwellings and recently by the new Court House in Brooklyn.

    Manufactured for the **American Iron Blind Company** *and orders received for the same by the* **Architectural Iron Works, 42 Duane Street, New York.**

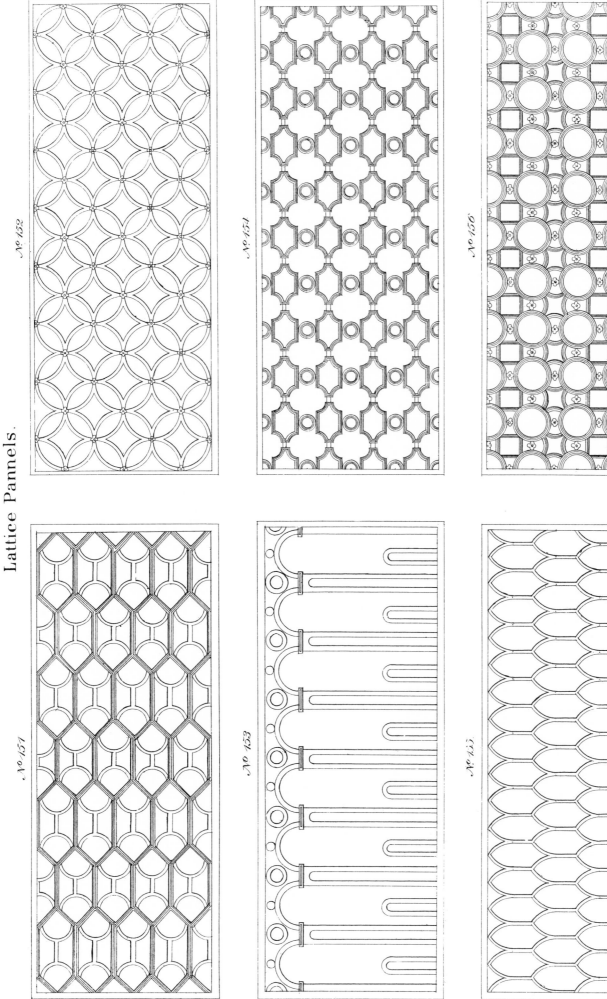

Plate LVII.

Lattice Pannels.

Nº 152

Nº 154

Nº 156

Nº 151

Nº 153

Nº 155

ARCHITECTURAL IRON WORKS – NEW YORK.

Lith. of Sarony Major & Knapp, 449 Broadway N.Y.

Plate LVIII.

JOHN C. GRAY ESQ, BOSTON.

No: 11.

Lith of Sarony, Major & Knapp, 449 Broadway NY

ARCHITECTURAL IRON WORKS,—NEW-YORK.

Plate LIX.

Elevation of H.H.Honnewell's Building, Boston.
No: 12.

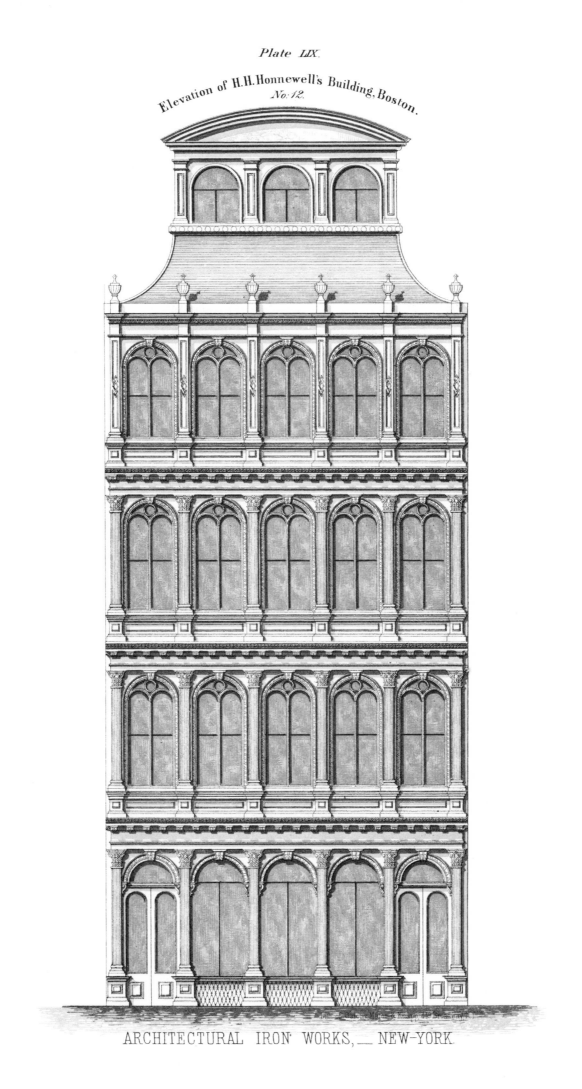

ARCHITECTURAL IRON WORKS,__ NEW-YORK.

Plate LX.

Elevation of Grain Building.

No: 27.

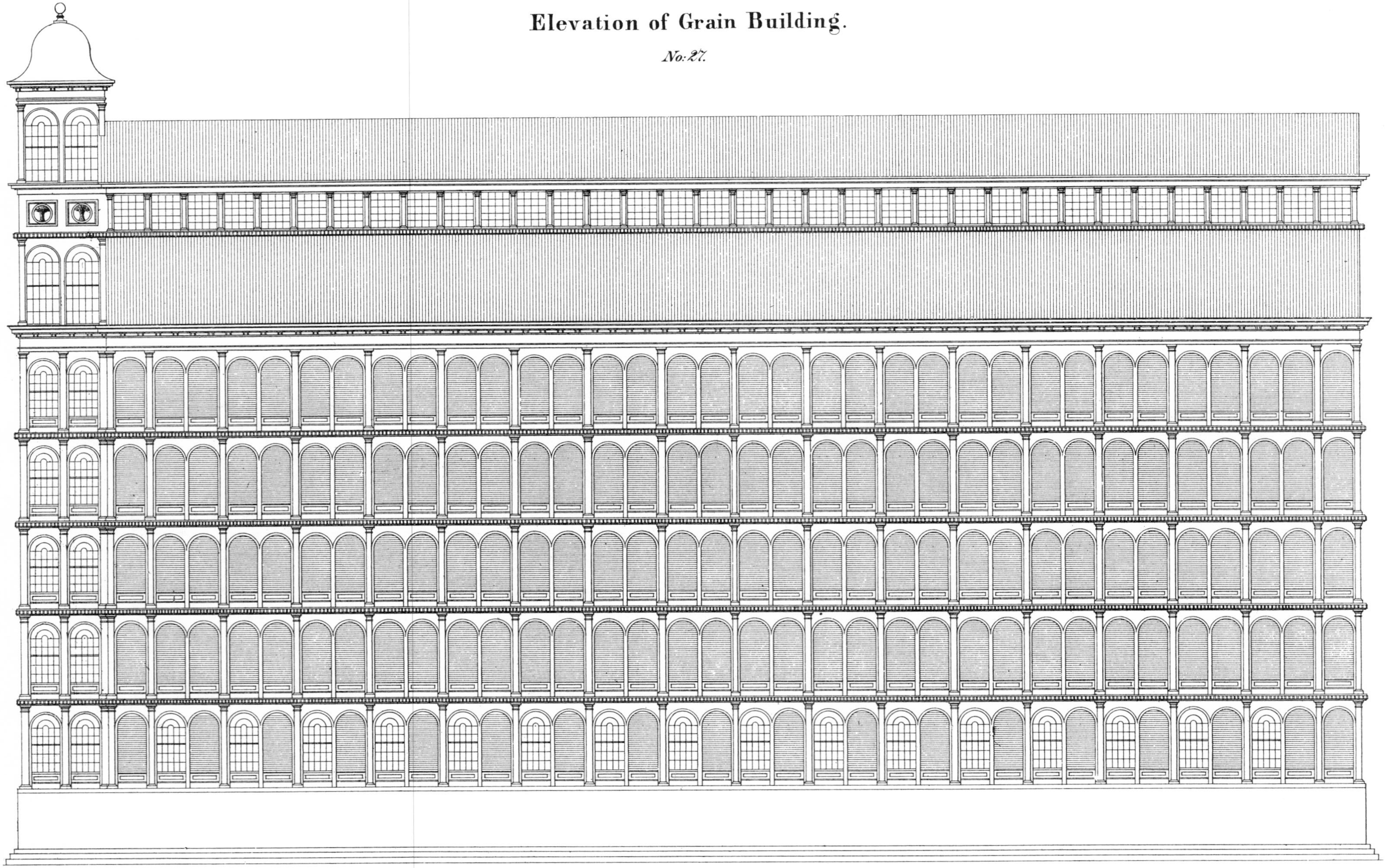

Lith. of Sarony,Major & Knapp. 443 Broadway, N.Y.

ARCHITECTURAL IRON WORKS,—NEW-YORK

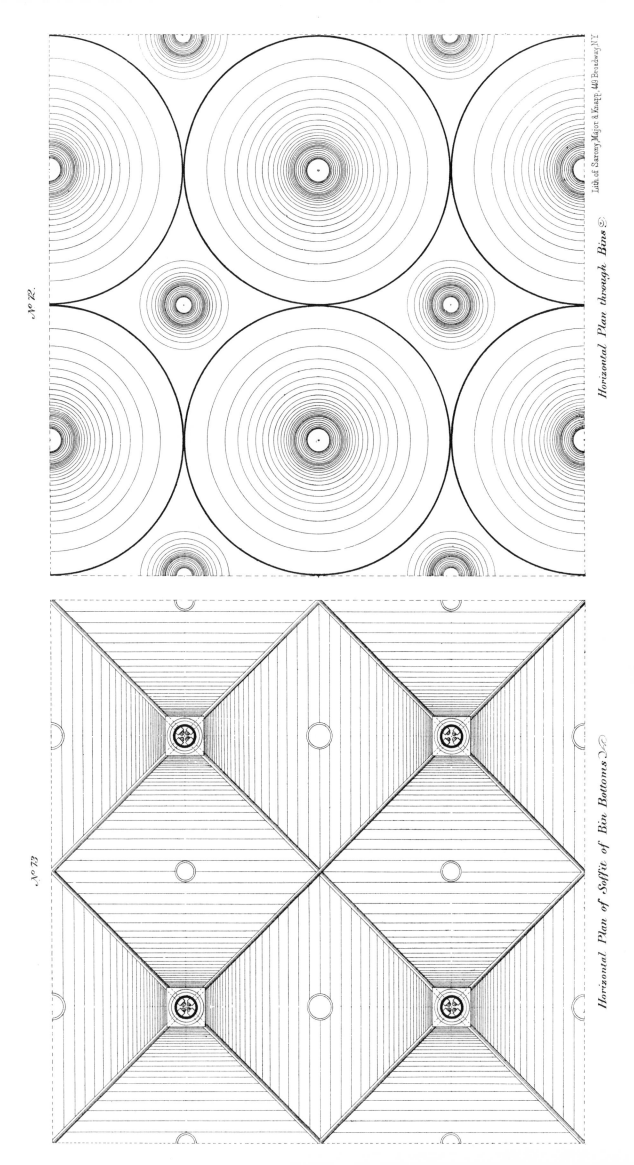

Plate LXI.

Details of Grain Building.

Nº 72.

Nº 73

Lith. of Sarony, Major & Knapp, 449 Broadway, N.Y.

Horizontal Plan through Bins.

Horizontal Plan of Soffit of Bin Bottoms.

ARCHITECTURAL . IRON WORKS, _ NEW-YORK.

Plate LXII.
Section of Grain Building through Bins.
No. 71

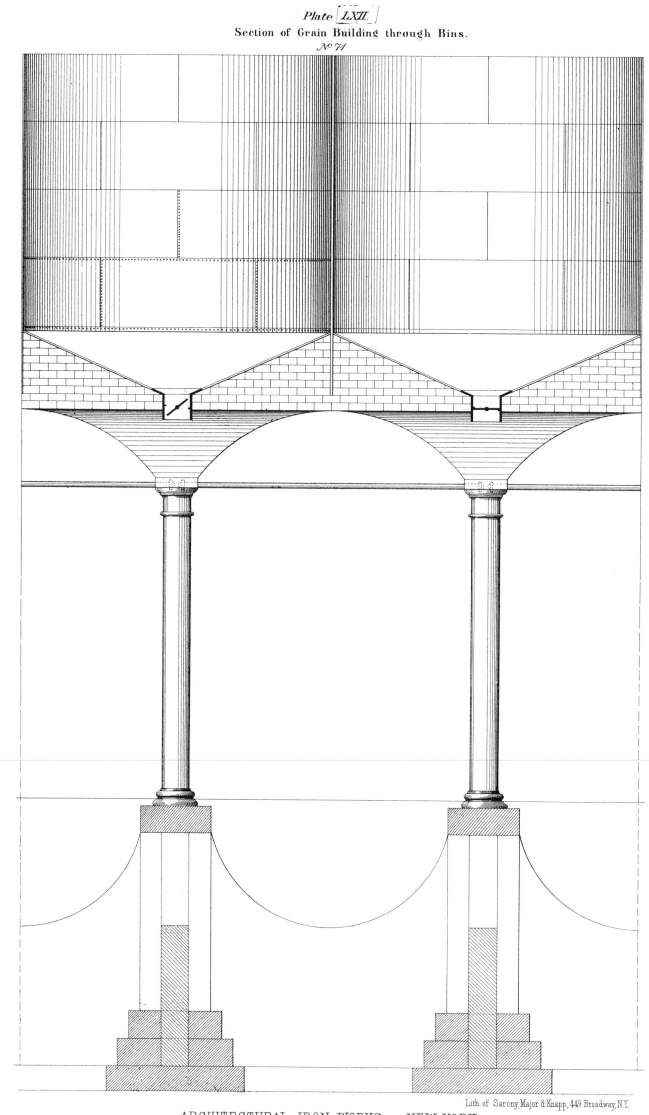

ARCHITECTURAL IRON WORKS, — NEW-YORK.

Plate LXIII.

Tension Rod Girders. No. 271.

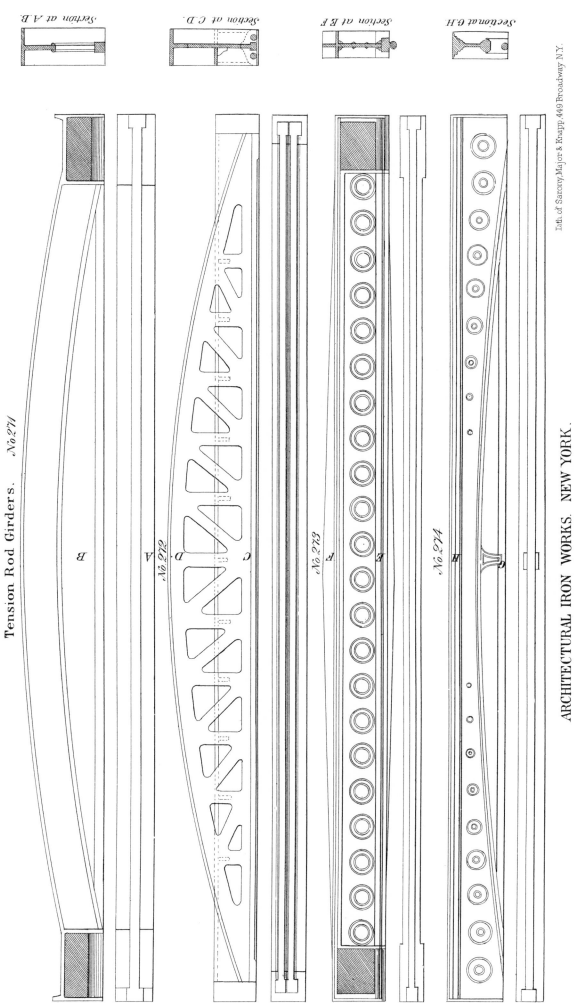

Section at A.B.

Section at C.D.

Section at E.F.

Section at G.H.

No. 272.

No. 273.

No. 274.

ARCHITECTURAL IRON WORKS. NEW YORK.

Lith. of Sarony, Major & Knapp. 449 Broadway N.Y.

Plate LXIV.

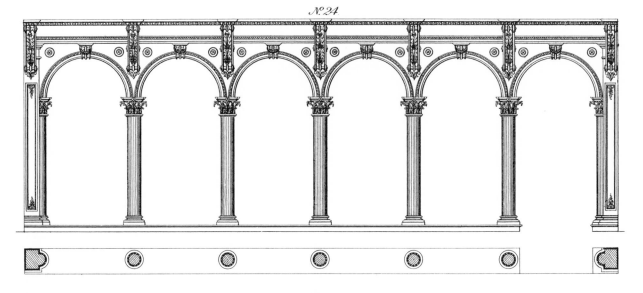

Nº 25

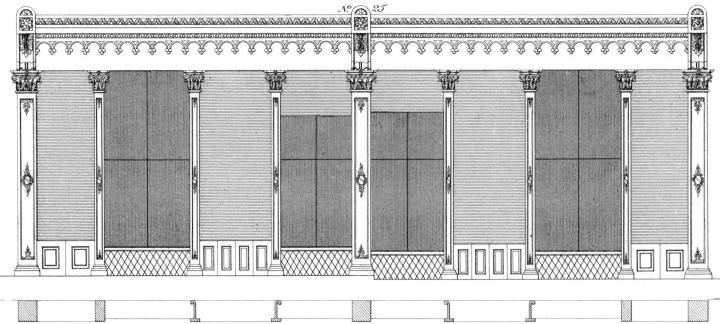

Nº 26

Lith. of Sarony, Major & Knapp, 449 Broadway, N.Y.

ARCHITECTURAL IRON WORKS,_NEW-YORK.

Plate LXV.
No.23.

ARCHITECTURAL IRON WORKS,—NEW-YORK.

Lith of Sarony, Major & Knapp, 449 Broadway, N.Y.

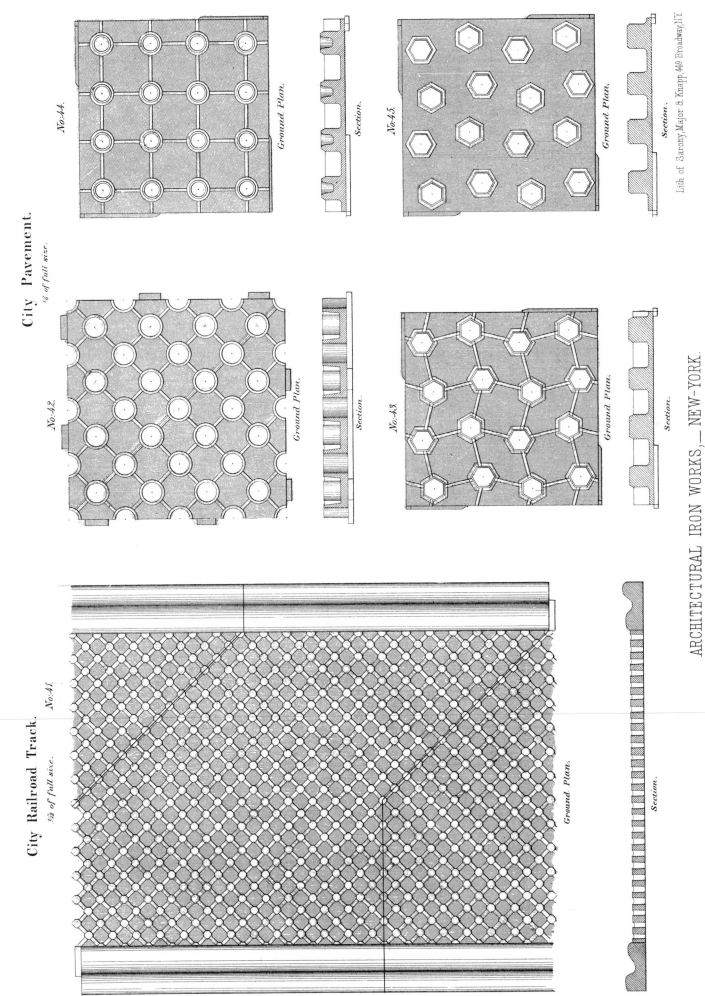

Plate LXVI.

City Pavement.
⅙ of full size.

No. 44.
Ground Plan.
Section.

No. 45.
Ground Plan.
Section.

No. 42.
Ground Plan.
Section.

No. 43.
Ground Plan.
Section.

City Railroad Track.
½ of full size.

No. 41.
Ground Plan.
Section.

Lith. of Sarony, Major & Knapp, 449 Broadway, N.Y.

ARCHITECTURAL IRON WORKS,— NEW-YORK.

Plate LXVII.
Elevation for Banking House & Office.
No: 22.

Lith. of Sarony, Major & Knapp, 449 Broadway, N.Y.

ARCHITECTURAL IRON WORKS NEW YORK

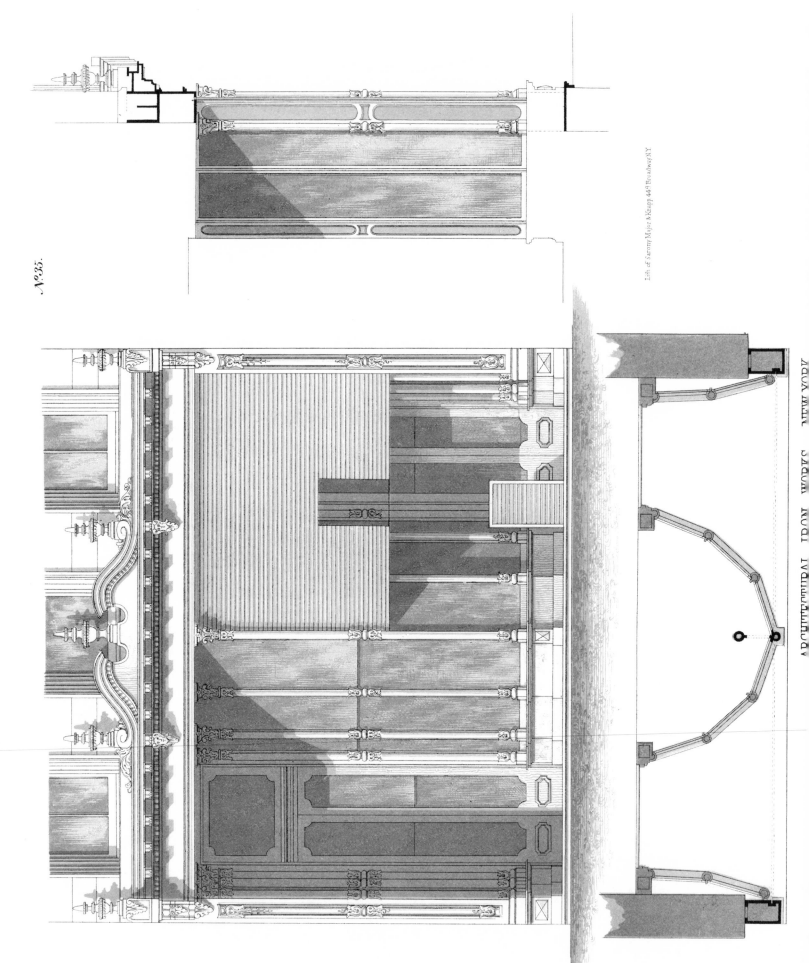

Plate LXVIII.

Nº 35.

ARCHITECTURAL IRON WORKS, NEW YORK.

Lith. of Sarony Major & Knapp 449 Broadway N.Y.

Plate LXIX.

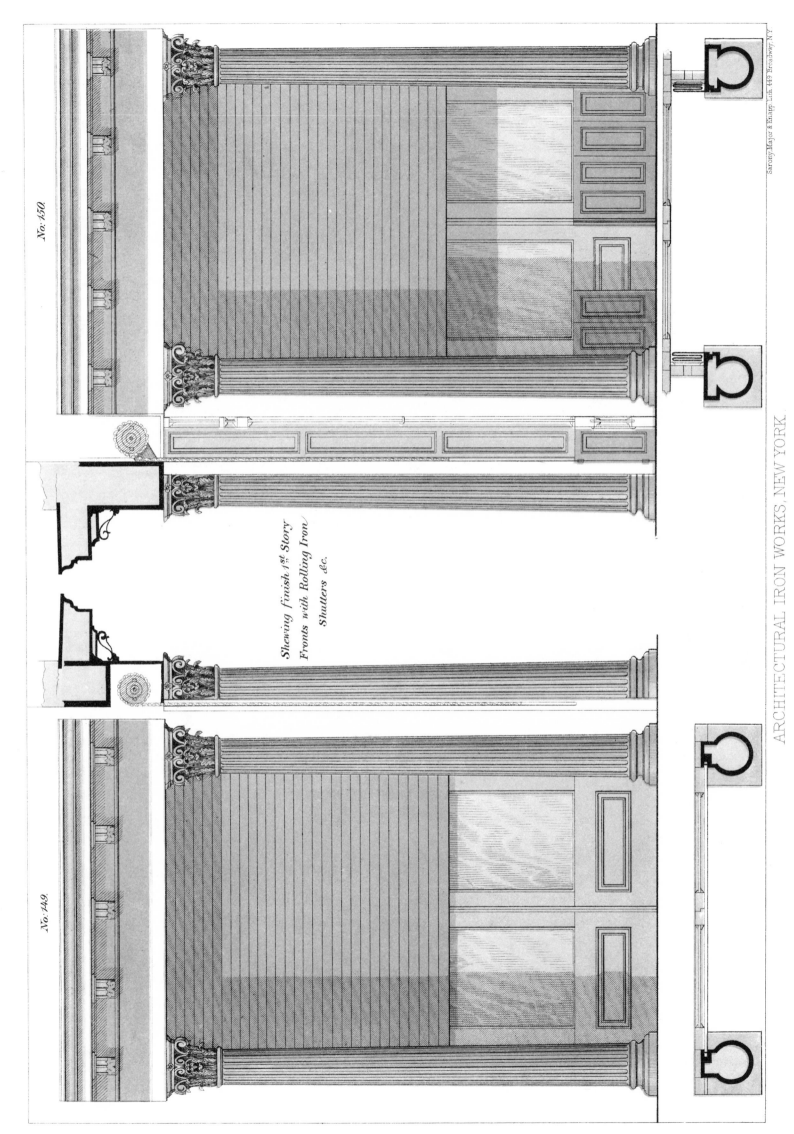

No: 150.

No: 149.

Shewing finish 1st Story Fronts with Rolling Iron Shutters &c.

Sarony Major & Knapp Lith 449 Broadway N.Y.

ARCHITECTURAL IRON WORKS, NEW YORK.

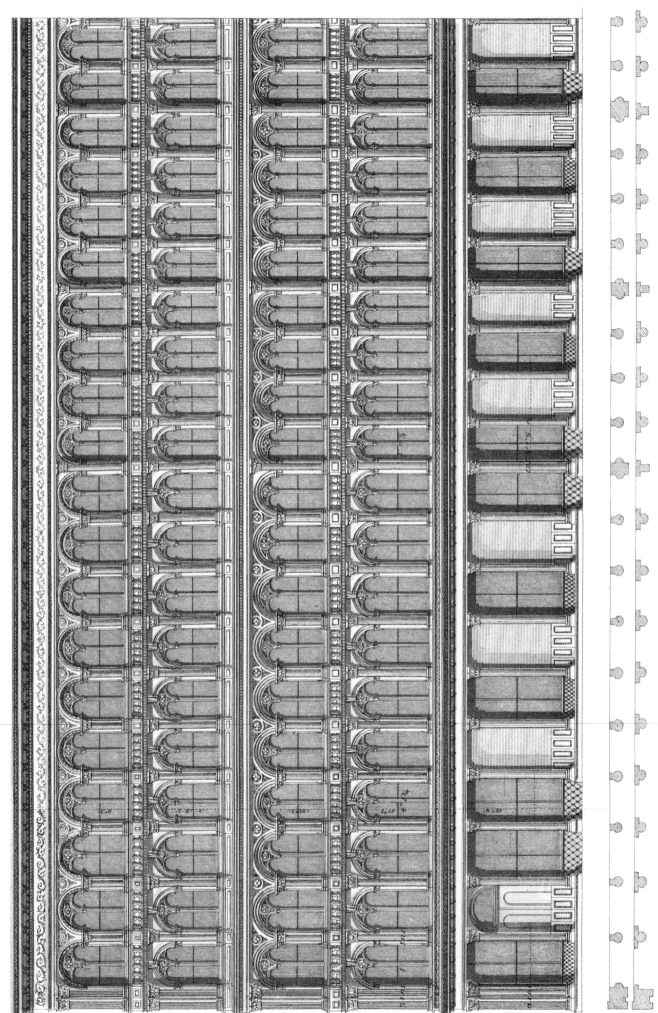

Plate LXX.

Front Elevation for Fred.Tuttle and others   Chicago Ills.

No:28.

Scale one inch to twelve feet

ARCHITECTURAL IRON WORKS NEW YORK

Lith of Sarony Major & Knapp, 449 Broadway

Plate LXXI.

Details : Rolling Iron Shutters .

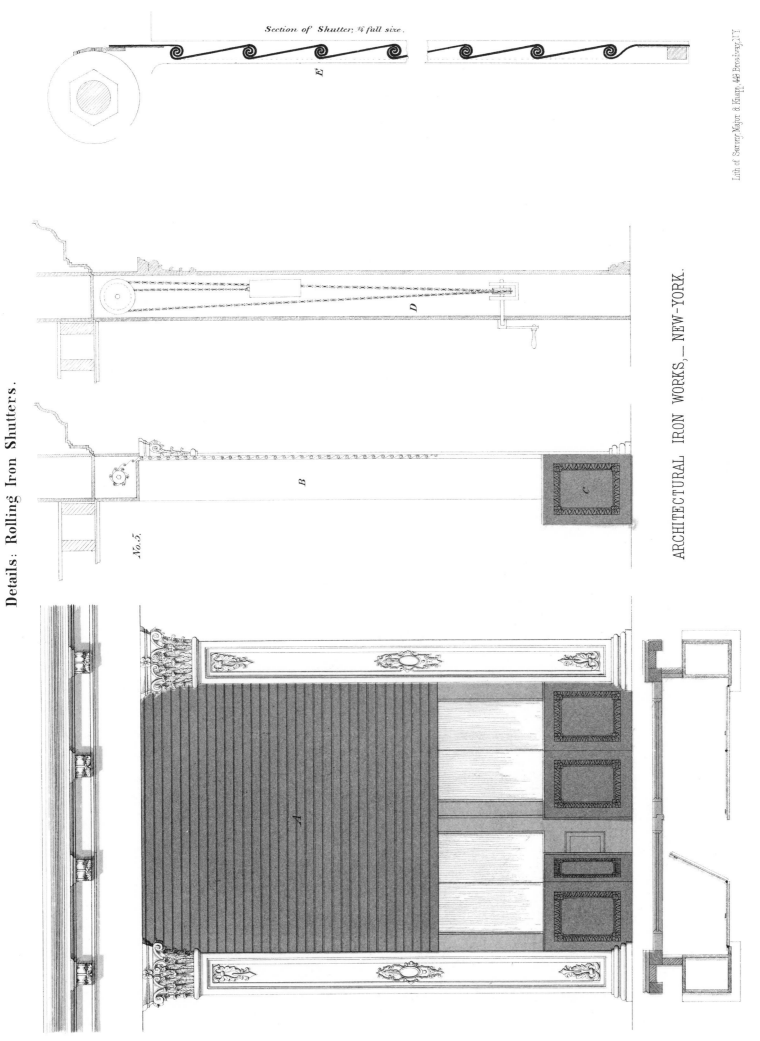

Section of Shutter; ¼ full size.

E

No. 5.

B

C

D

A

Lith of Sarony Major & Knapp, 449 Broadway, N.Y.

ARCHITECTURAL IRON WORKS,— NEW-YORK.

Plate LXXII.

Consoles Brackets & Rosett's.

No. 33. No. 36. No. 37. No. 39. No. 40. No. 13. No. 12. No. 11. No. 10. No. 16. No. 14. No. 9. No. 15. No. 56. No. 54. No. 66. No. 69. No. 55. No. 57. No. 65. No. 72. No. 59. No. 60. No. 63. No. 64. No. 74. No. 75.

Lith. of Sarony, Major & Knapp, 449 Broadway, N.Y.

ARCHITECTURAL IRON WORKS,__NEW-YORK.

Plate LXXIII.

Sugar Shed for Havana, Cuba.

No:19.

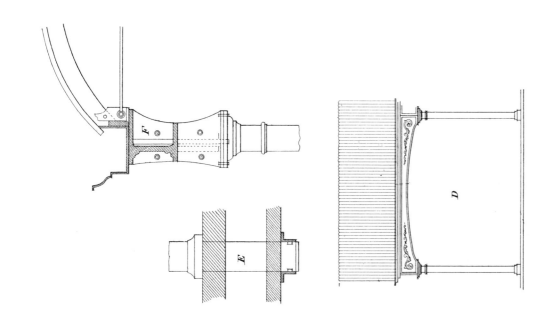

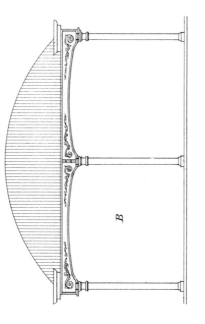

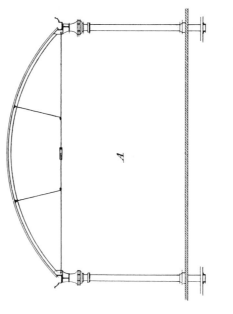

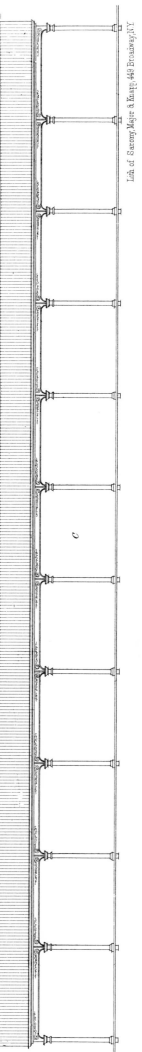

ARCHITECTURAL IRON WORKS,—NEW-YORK

Plate LXXIV

N.º 36.

BILLING & Co.

ARCHITECTURAL IRON WORKS — NEW-YORK.

Plate LXXV

Nº 38

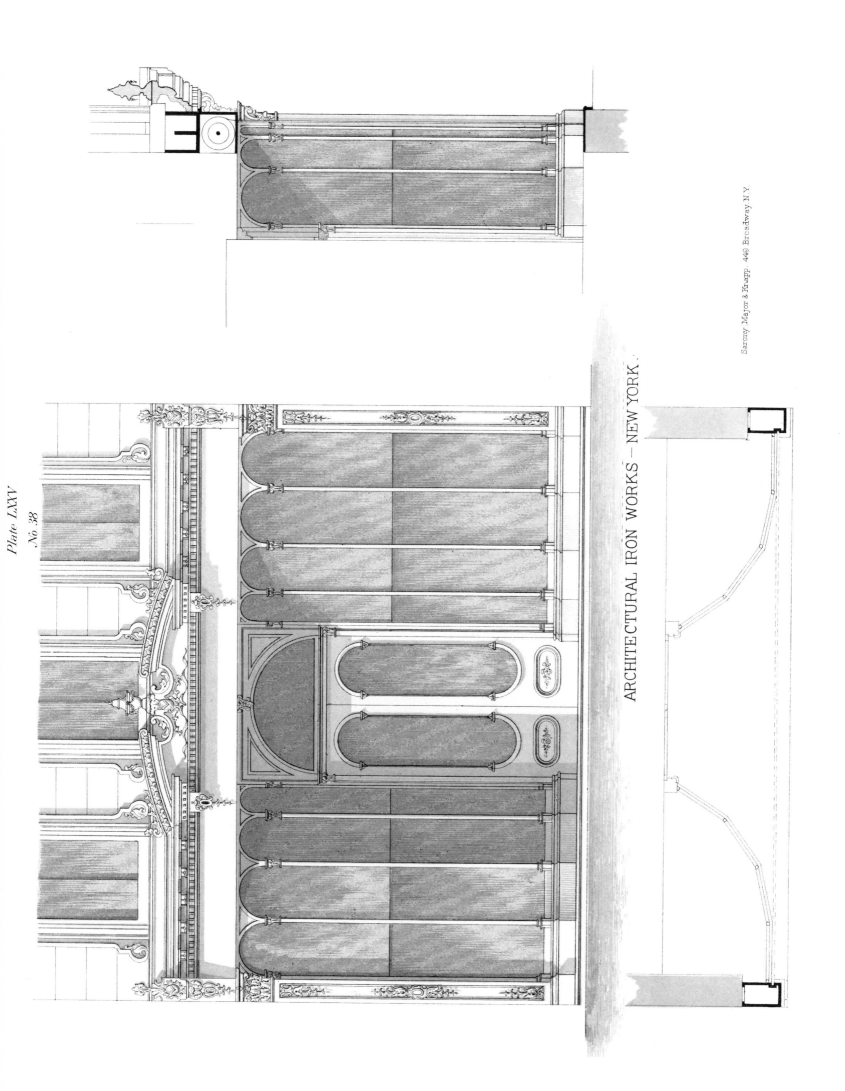

ARCHITECTURAL IRON WORKS – NEW YORK.

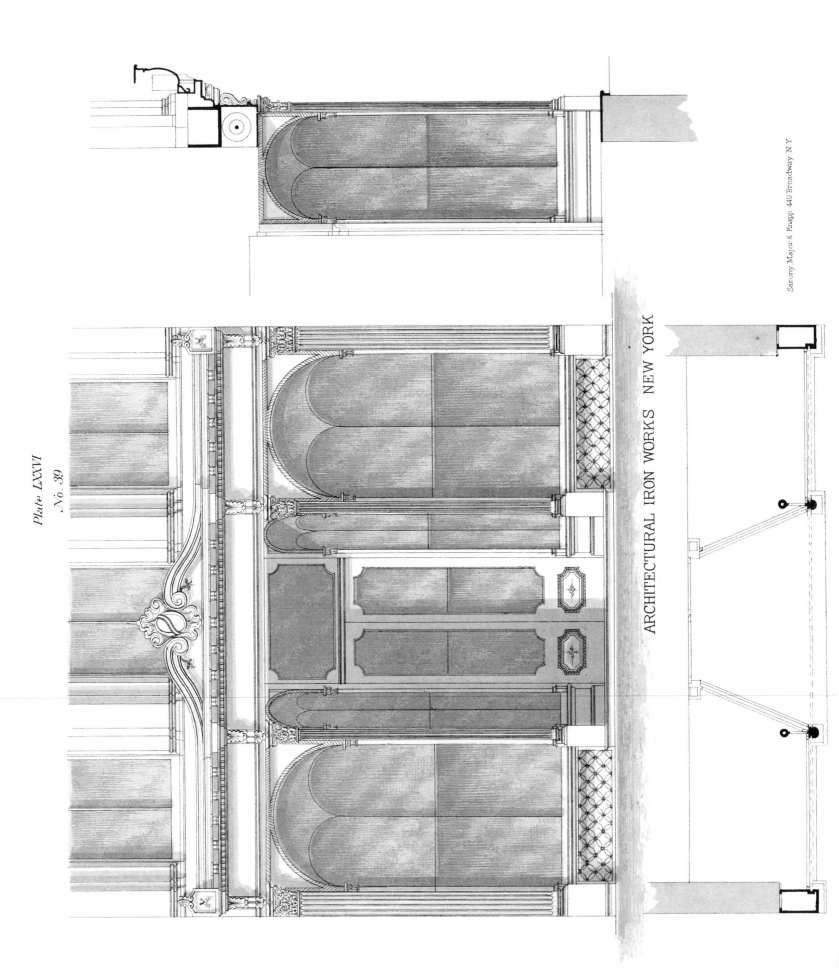

Plate LXXVI

Nò. 39

ARCHITECTURAL IRON WORKS   NEW YORK

Sarony Major & Knapp 449 Broadway N.Y

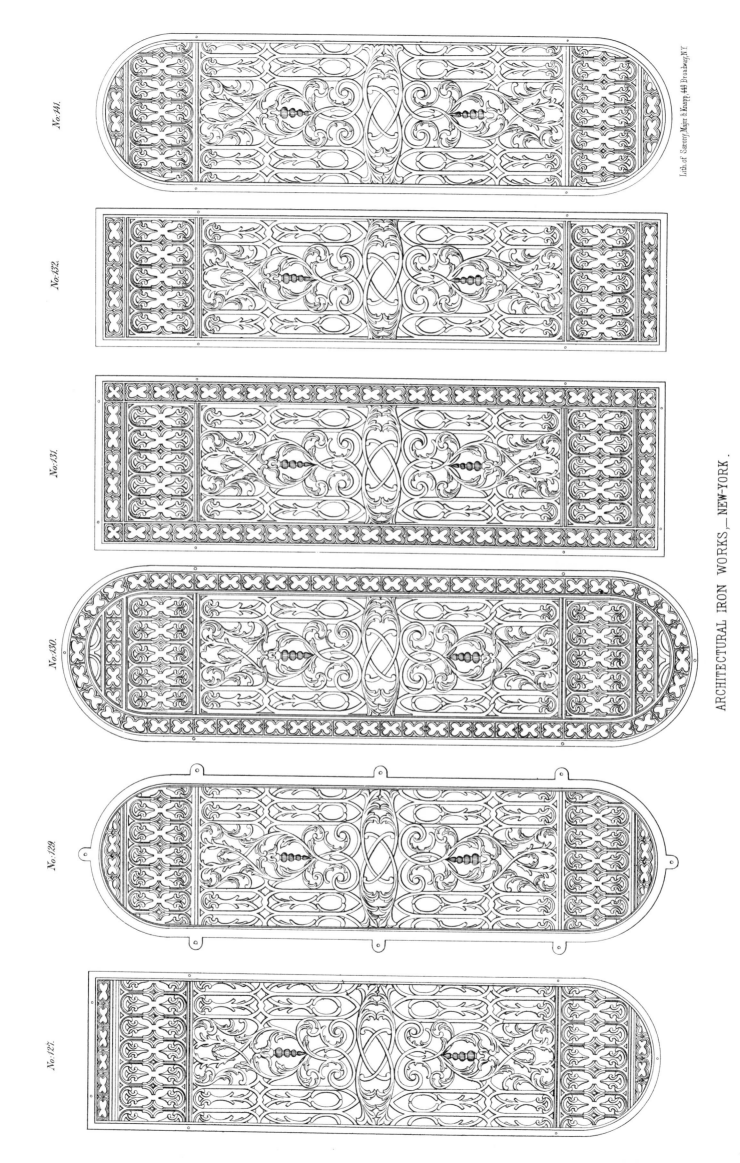

Plate LXXVII.

No. 141.

No. 132.

No. 131.

No. 130.

No. 129.

No. 127.

Lith. of Sarony, Major & Knapp, 449 Broadway, N.Y.

ARCHITECTURAL IRON WORKS,—NEW-YORK.

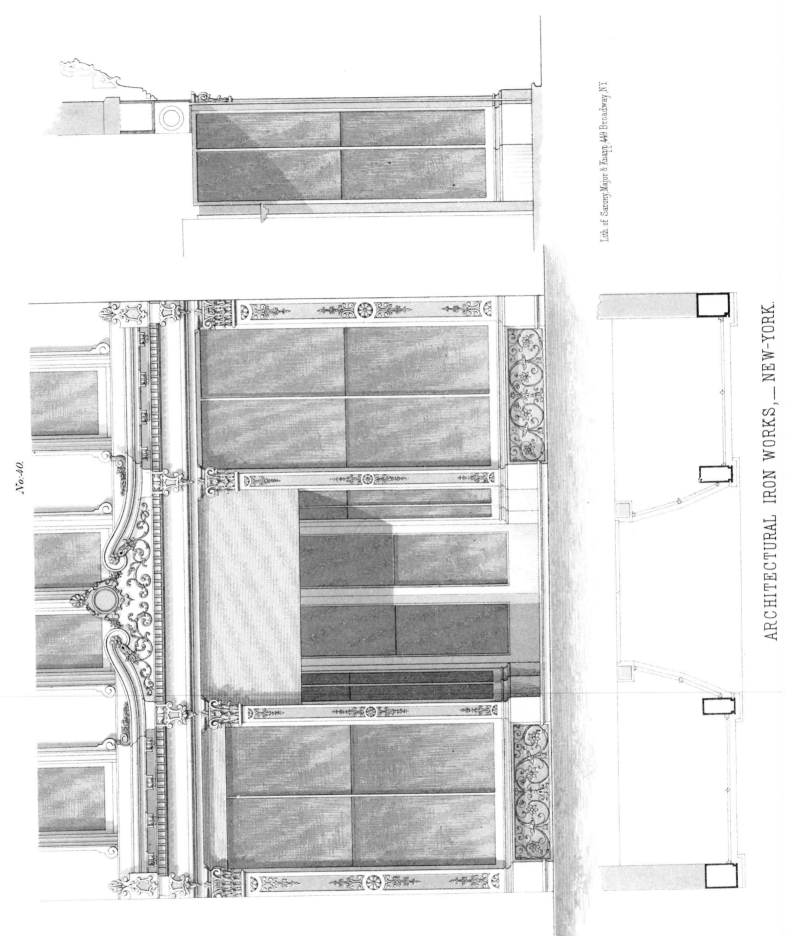

Plate LXVIII.

No. 40.

Lith. of Sarony,Major & Knapp 449 Broadway,N.Y

ARCHITECTURAL IRON WORKS,— NEW-YORK.

Plate LXXIX.

ARCHITECTURAL IRON WORKS. __ NEW-YORK.

Lith. of Sarony Major & Knapp, 449 Broadway, N.Y.

No: 163.

1' 1"

5½"

No: 164.

2' 3"

1' 4"

Plate LXXX

No: 165.

3' 10"

1' 7"

No: 166.

3' 8"

11"

No: 167.

2' 2"

9"

No: 168.

1' 8"

8½"

No: 169.

2' 4"

1' 2"

No: 170.

3' 0"

10"

No: 171.

4' 0"

1' 6"

No: 172.

2' 9"

8"

Lith. of Sarony, Major & Knapp, 449 Broadway, N.Y.

ARCHITECTURAL IRON WORKS,—NEW-YORK.

Plate LXXXI.

No: 176.

No: 175.

Lith. of Sarony, Major & Knapp. 449 Broadway, N.Y.

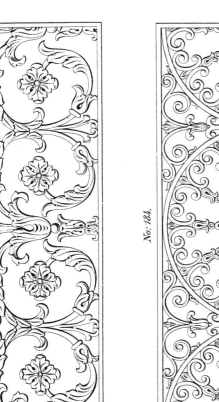

No: 183.

No: 184.

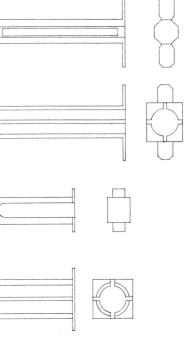

No: 182.

No: 181.

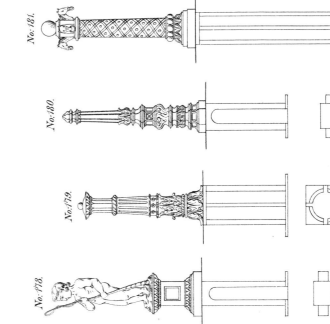

No: 180.

No: 179.

No: 178.

No: 177.

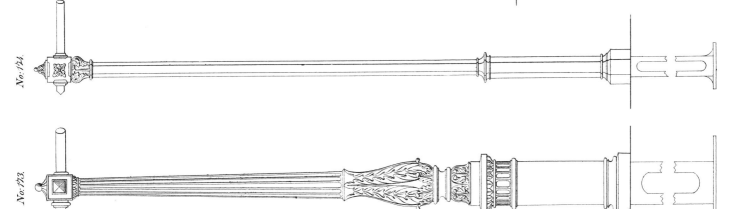

No: 174.

No: 173.

ARCHITECTURAL IRON WORKS,— NEW-YORK.

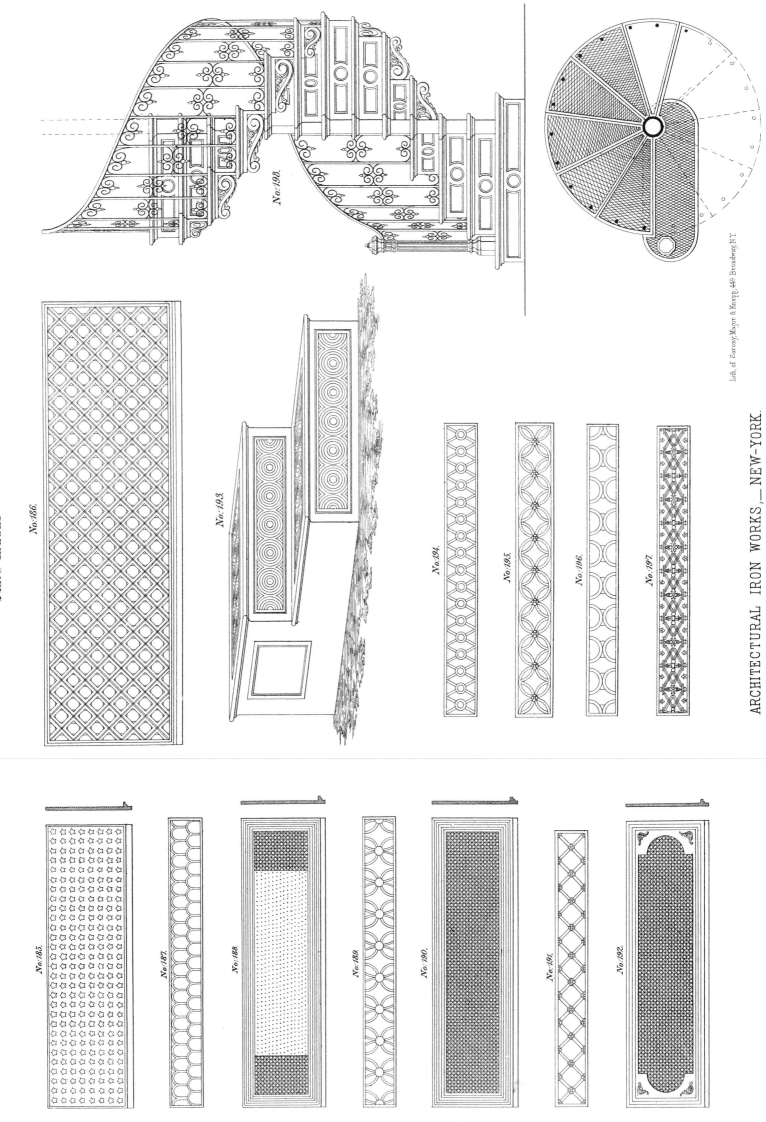

Plate LXXXII

No. 185.

No. 186.

No. 187.

No. 188.

No. 189.

No. 190.

No. 191.

No. 192.

No. 193.

No. 194.

No. 195.

No. 196.

No. 197.

No. 198.

ARCHITECTURAL IRON WORKS,—NEW-YORK.

Lith. of Sarony, Major & Knapp, 449 Broadway, NY

Plate LXXIII.

Elevation & Section of Sidewalk &c, Shewing Vault under Street.

No:45.

ARCHITECTURAL IRON WORKS,— NEW-YORK.

Lith of Sarony, Major & Knapp, 449 Broadway, NY

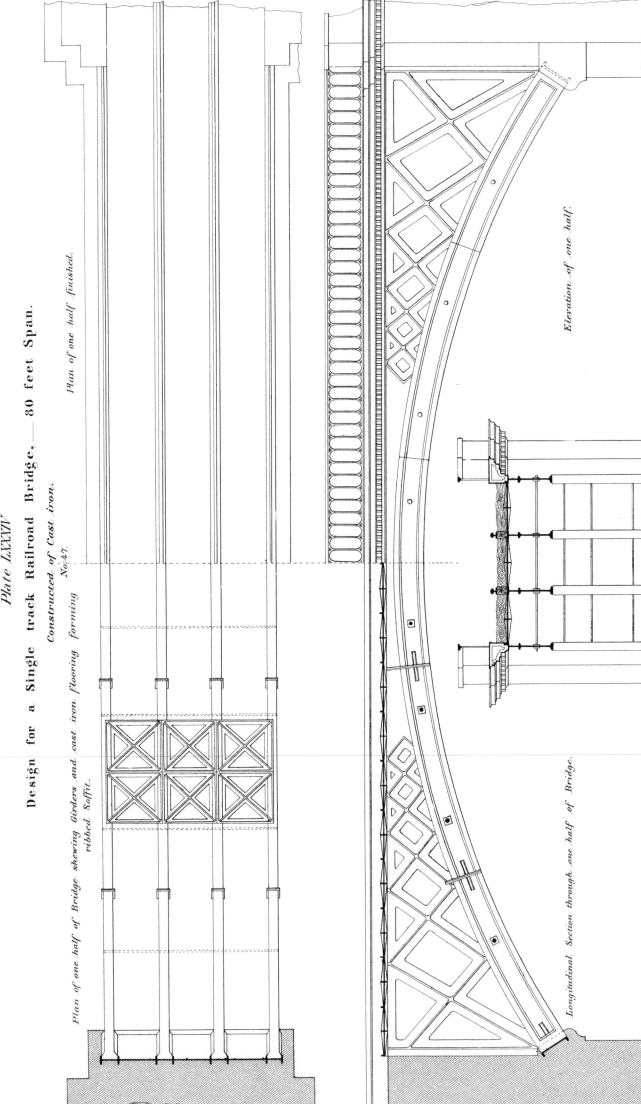

Plate LXXIV

Design for a Single track Railroad Bridge,— 80 feet Span.

Constructed of Cast iron.

No: 47.

Plan of one half finished.

Plan of one half of Bridge shewing Girders and cast iron flooring forming ribbed Soffit.

Elevation of one half.

Longitudinal Section through one half of Bridge.

Transverse Section through crown of Arch.

Scale, ⅛ of an inch to a foot.

Lith. of Sarony, Major & Knapp, 449 Brdway, N.Y.

ARCHITECTURAL IRON WORKS,— NEW-YORK.

Plate LXXXV

Design for a Single Track Railroad Bridge,—— 50 feet Span.

No. 49.

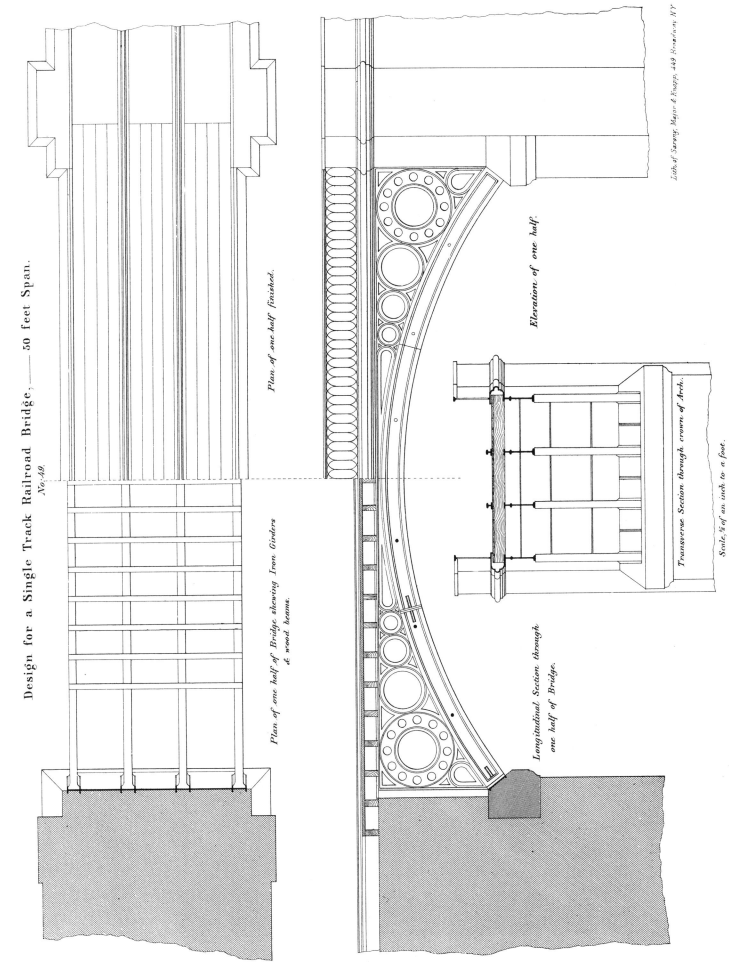

Plan of one half finished.

Plan of one half of Bridge shewing Iron Girders & wood beams.

Elevation of one half.

Transverse Section through crown of Arch.

Longitudinal Section through one half of Bridge.

Scale, ⅛ of an inch to a foot.

Lith. of Sarony, Major & Knapp, 449 Broadway N.Y.

ARCHITECTURAL IRON WORKS,—— NEW-YORK.

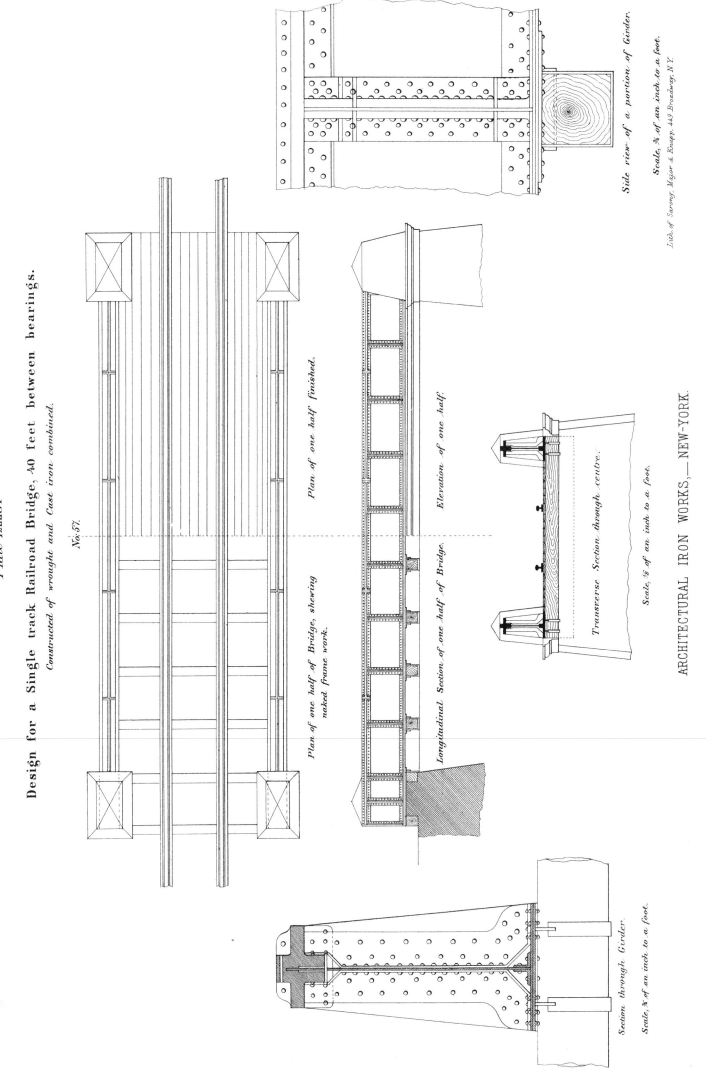

Plate LXXVI

Design for a Single track Railroad Bridge, 40 feet between bearings.

Constructed of wrought and Cast iron combined.

No. 57.

Plan of one half finished.

Plan of one half of Bridge, shewing naked frame work.

Elevation of one half.

Longitudinal Section of one half of Bridge.

Side view of a portion of Girder.

Scale, ¾ of an inch to a foot.

Lith. of Sarony, Major & Knapp, 449 Broadway, N.Y.

Transverse Section through centre.

Scale, ⅝ of an inch to a foot.

Section through Girder.

Scale, ¾ of an inch to a foot.

ARCHITECTURAL IRON WORKS,— NEW-YORK.

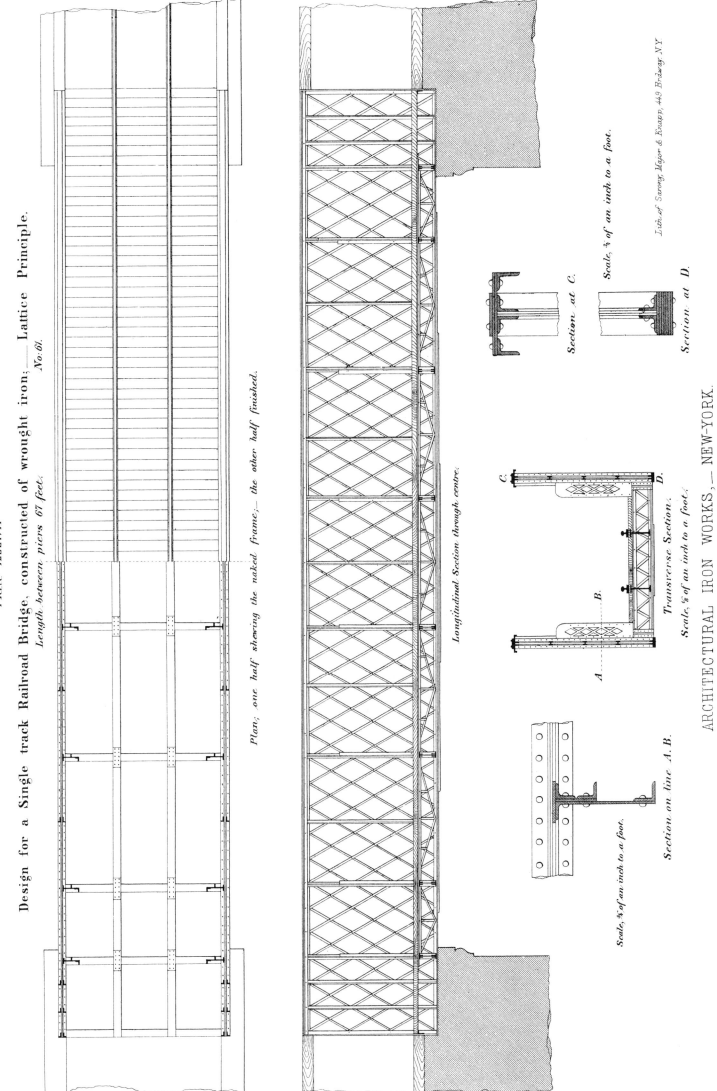

Plate LXXVII

Design for a Single track Railroad Bridge, constructed of wrought iron;— Lattice Principle.

No: 61.

Length between piers 67 feet.

Plan; one half showing the naked frame;— the other half finished.

Longitudinal Section through centre.

Section at C.

Scale, ⅓ of an inch to a foot.

Section at D.

Lith: of Sarony, Major & Knapp, 449 Br'dway, N.Y.

C.   *D.*

A   *B.*

Transverse Section.

Scale, ⅛ of an inch to a foot.

Section on line A.B.

Scale, ¾ of an inch to a foot.

ARCHITECTURAL IRON WORKS,— NEW-YORK.

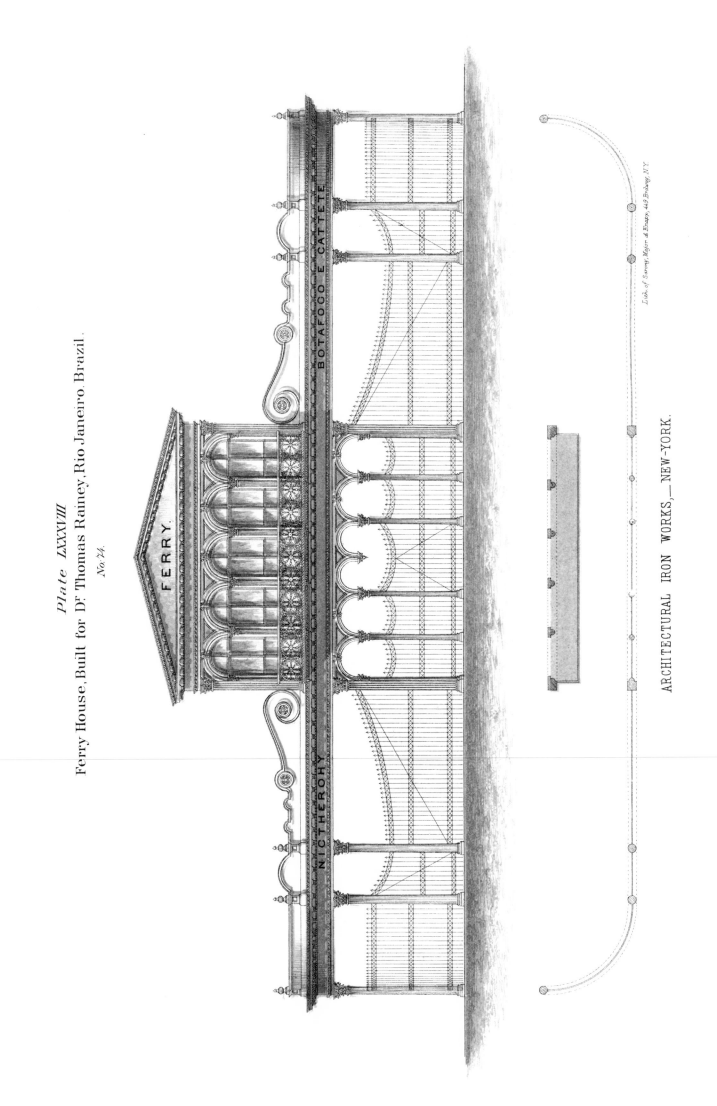

Plate LXXVIII

Ferry House, Built for Dr Thomas Rainey, Rio Janeiro. Brazil.

No. 74.

FERRY.

BOTAFOGO E CATTETE.

NICTHEROHY

Lith. of Sarony Major & Knapp, 449 Broadway, N.Y.

ARCHITECTURAL IRON WORKS,—NEW-YORK.

Plate LXXXIX

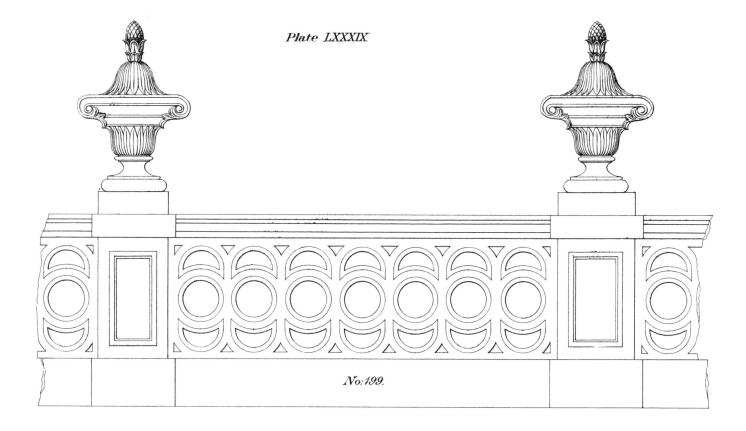

No: 199.

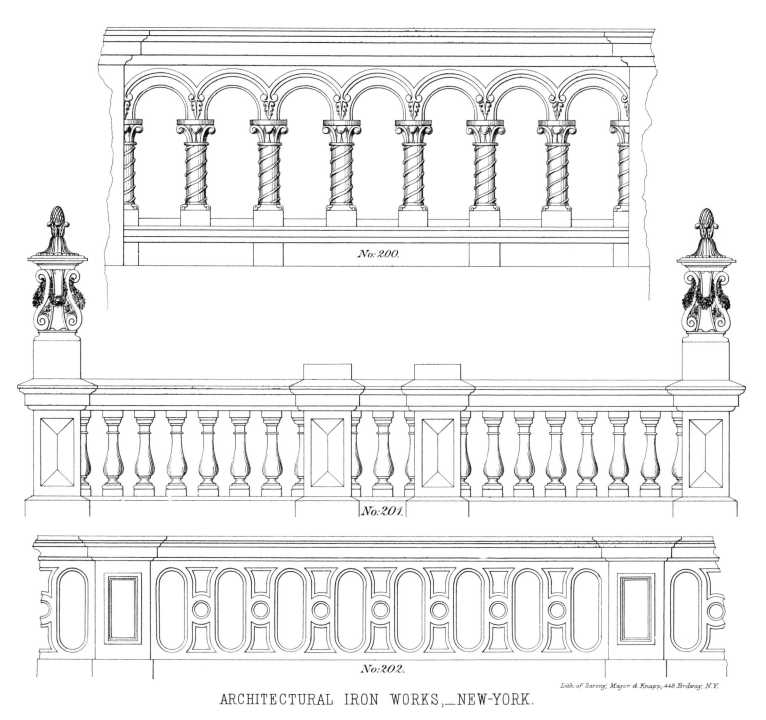

No: 200.

No: 201.

No: 202.

Lith. of Sarony, Major & Knapp, 449 Br'dway, N.Y.

ARCHITECTURAL IRON WORKS,—NEW-YORK.

Plate XC.

No: 14.

Lith. of Sarony, Major & Knapp, 449 Brdway N.Y.

ARCHITECTURAL IRON WORKS,___ NEW-YORK.

No: 203.

Plate XCI

No: 48.

No: 204.

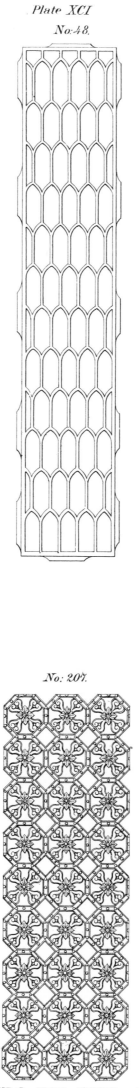

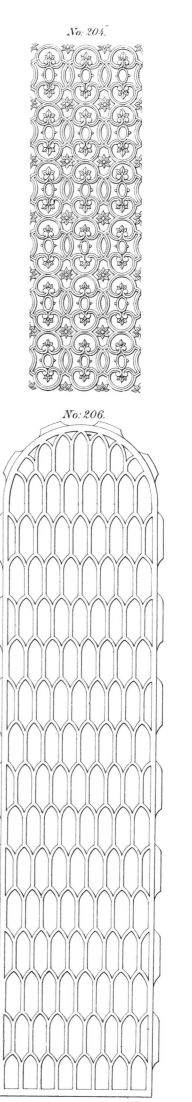

No: 206.

No: 205.

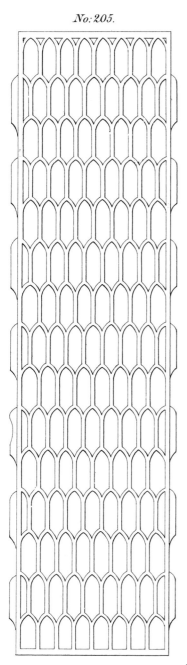

No: 207.

ARCHITECTURAL IRON WORKS,___NEW-YORK

Lith. of Sarony, Major & Knapp, 449 Brdway, N.Y.

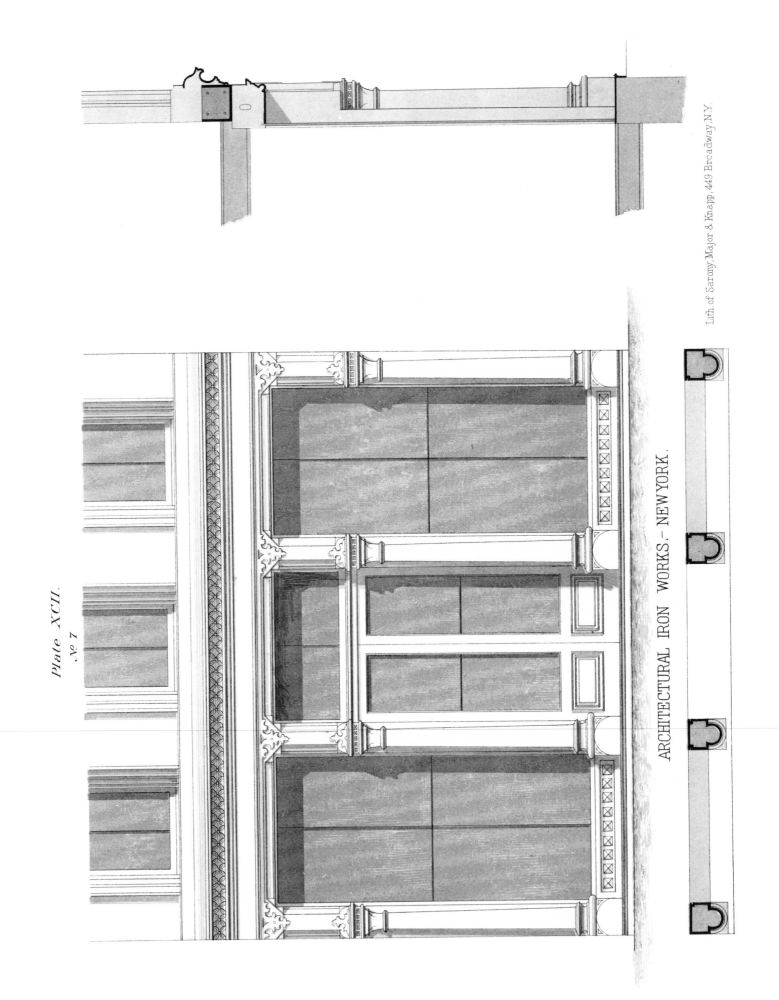

Plate XCII.

Nº 7

ARCHITECTURAL IRON WORKS.- NEW YORK.

Lith. of Sarony, Major & Knapp, 449 Broadway, N.Y.

Plate XCIII.

Nº 208

Nº 209

Nº 210

Nº 211

Nº 212

Nº 213

Nº 214

Nº 215

Nº 216

Nº 217

Nº 218

Nº 219

ARCHITECTURAL IRON WORKS,—NEW-YORK.

Lith. of Sarony, Major & Knapp, 449 Bd. wy N.Y.

Plate XCIV.

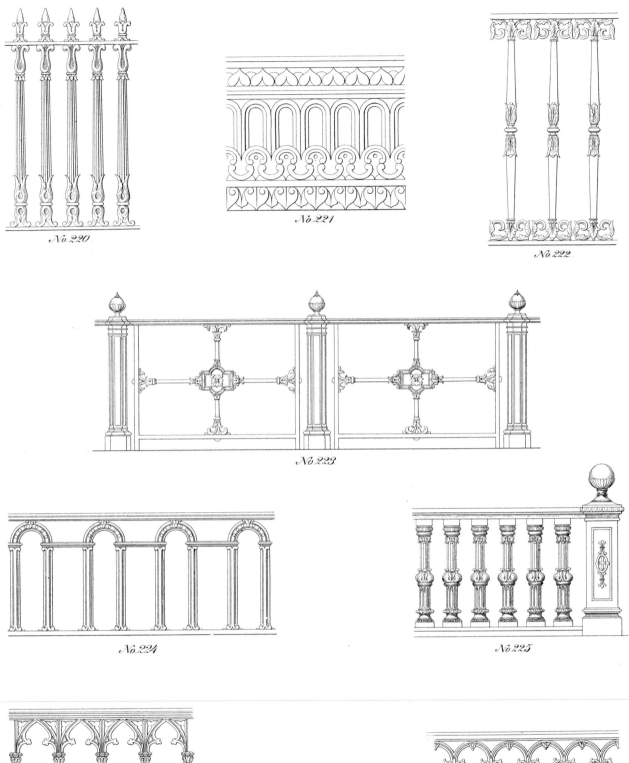

No 220

No 221

No 222

No 223

No 224

No 225

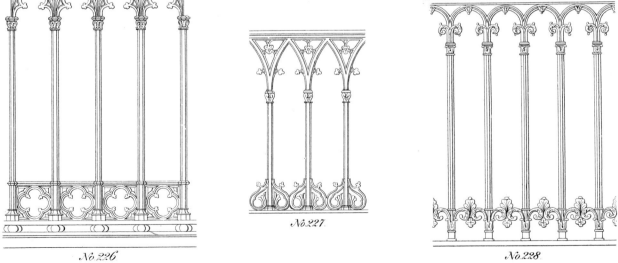

No 226

No 227

No 228

ARCHITECTURAL IRON WORKS — NEW YORK.

Lith. of Sarony, Major & Knapp, 449 Broadway N.Y.

Plate XCV.

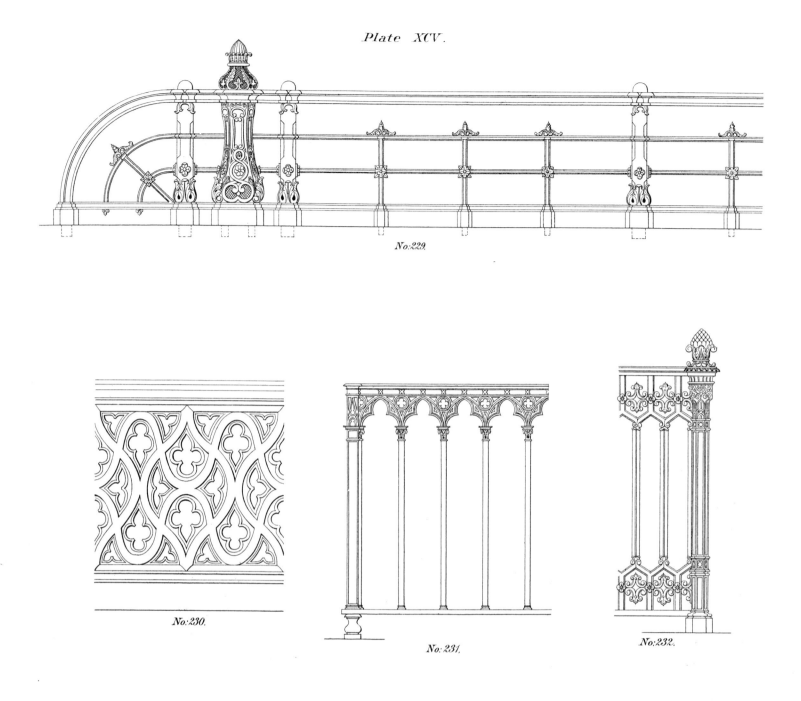

No:229.

No:230.

No:231.

No:232.

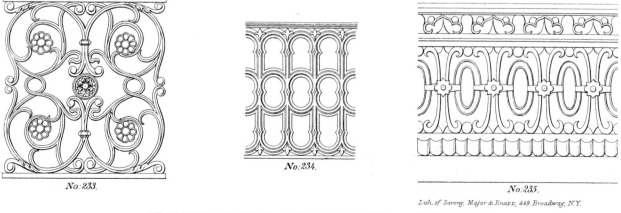

No:233.

No:234.

No:235.

Lith. of Sarony, Major & Knapp, 449 Broadway, N.Y.

ARCHITECTURAL IRON WORKS,— NEW-YORK.

Plate XCVI.

No: 236.

No: 237.

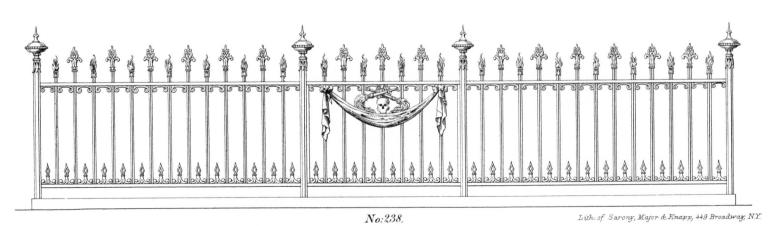

No: 238.

Lith. of Sarony, Major & Knapp, 449 Broadway, N.Y.

ARCHITECTURAL IRON WORKS,___ NEW-YORK.

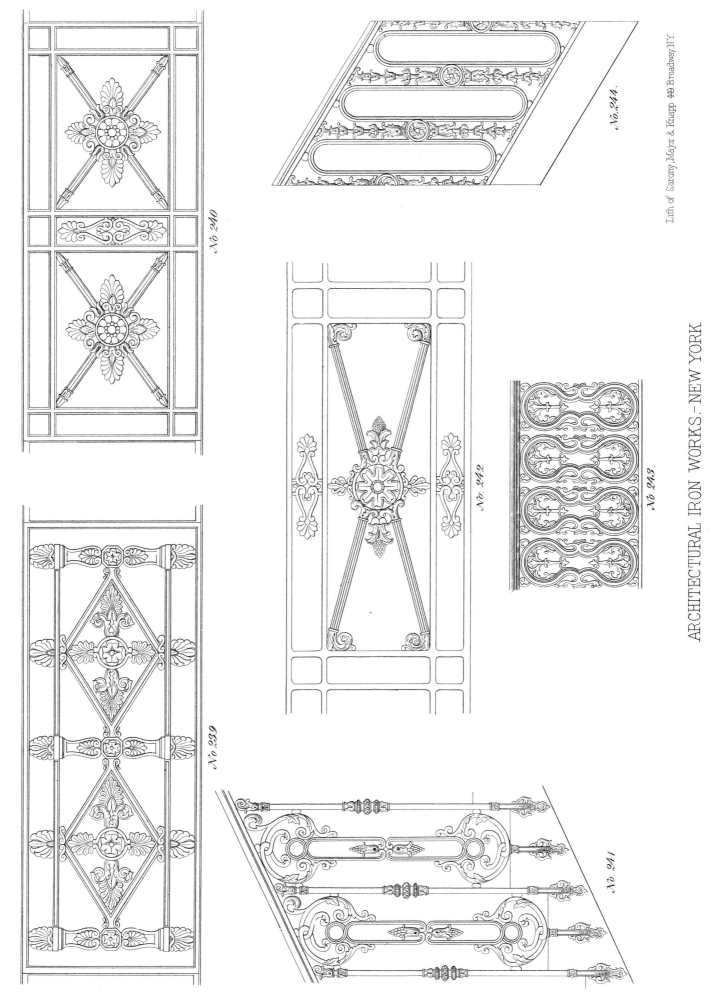

Plate XCVII.

No. 240

No. 239

No. 242

No. 243

No. 244.

No. 241

ARCHITECTURAL IRON WORKS.- NEW YORK

Lith of Sarony, Major & Knapp 449 Broadway N.Y.

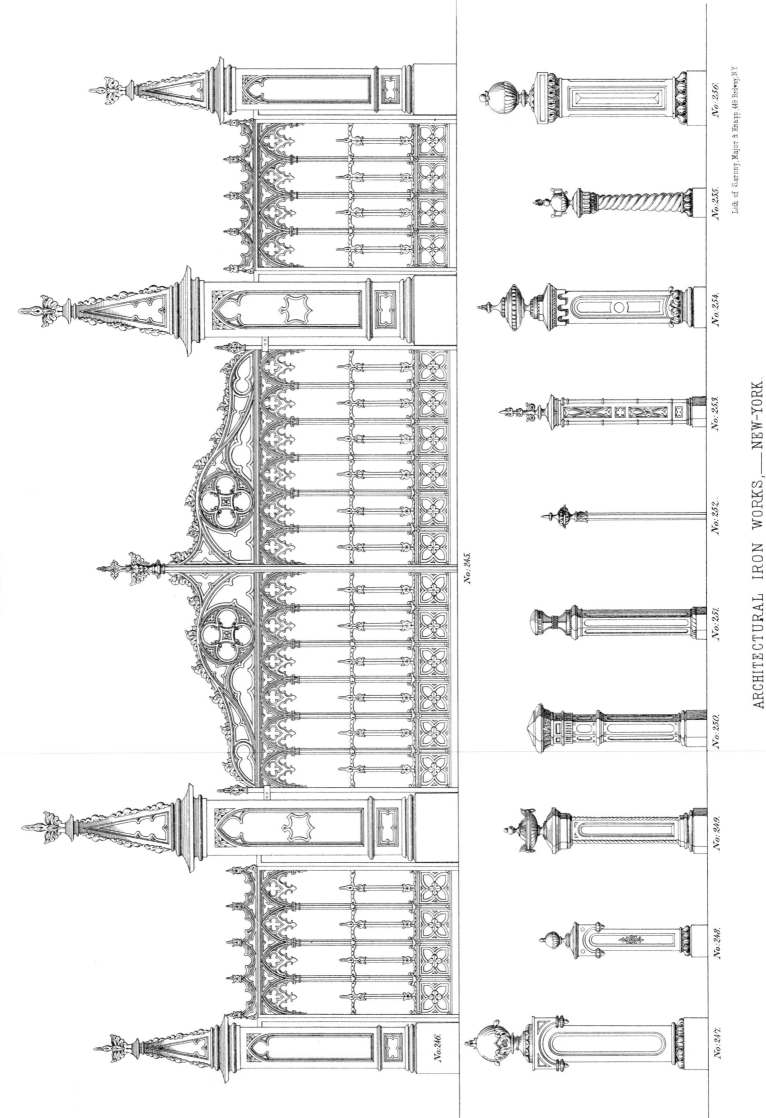

Plate XCVIII

No: 256.

No: 255.

No: 254.

No: 253.

No: 252.

No: 251.

No: 250.

No: 245.

No: 246.

No: 249.

No: 248.

No: 247.

ARCHITECTURAL IRON WORKS,——NEW-YORK.

Lith of Sarony, Major & Knapp, 449 B'dway, N.Y

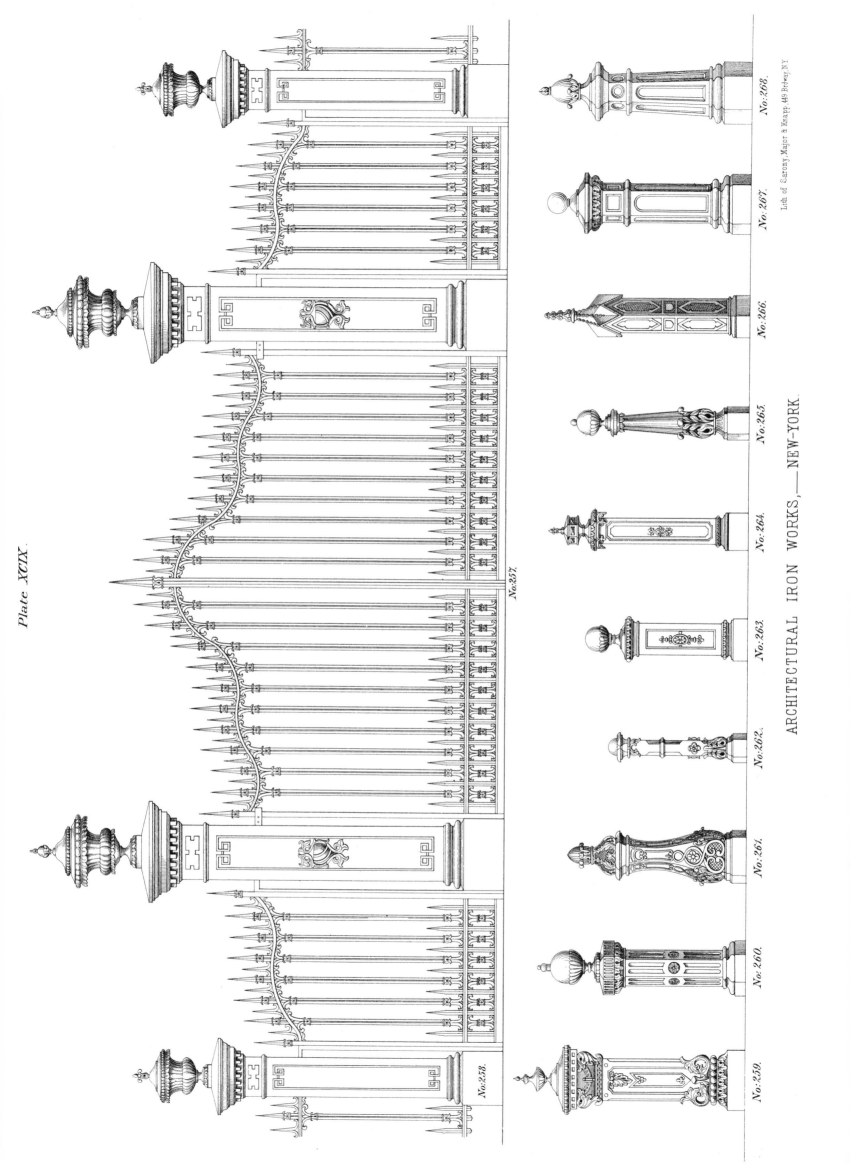

Plate XCIX.

No. 257.

No. 258.

No. 259.   No. 260.   No. 261.   No. 262.   No. 263.   No. 264.   No. 265.   No. 266.   No. 267.   No. 268.

ARCHITECTURAL IRON WORKS,—NEW-YORK.

Lith of Sarony, Major & Knapp. 449 Brdway, NY

Plate C.

No·105.

ARCHITECTURAL IRON WORKS,——NEW-YORK.

Plate CI.

No: 162

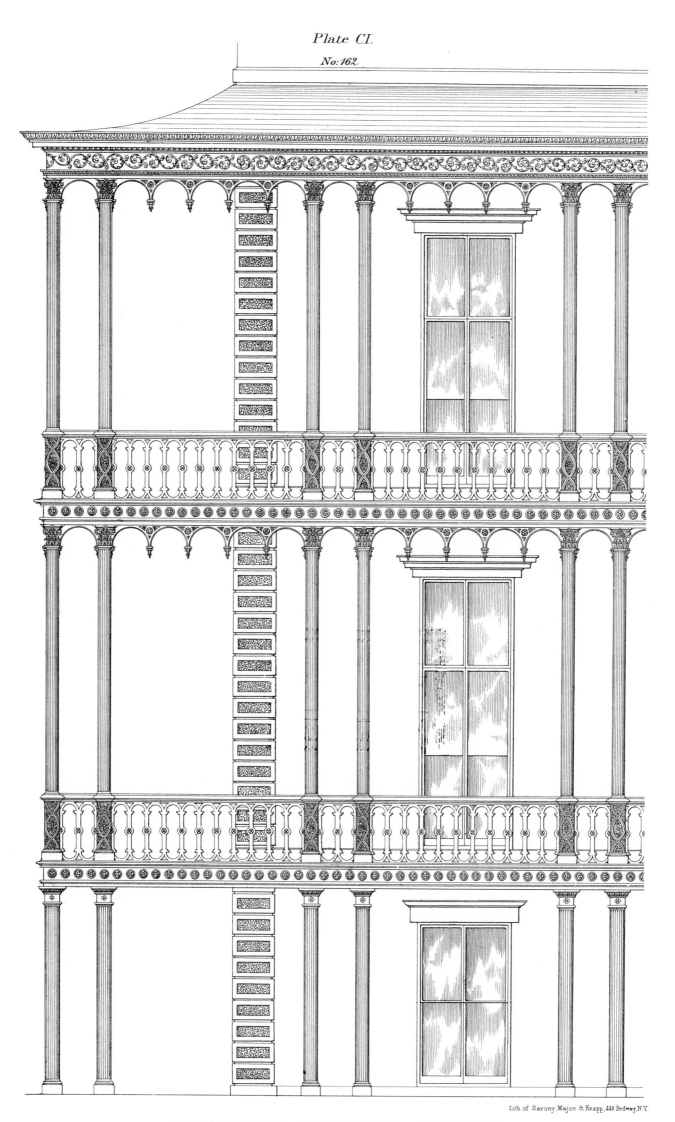

ARCHITECTURAL IRON WORKS, — NEW-YORK.

Plate CII.
Nº 75.

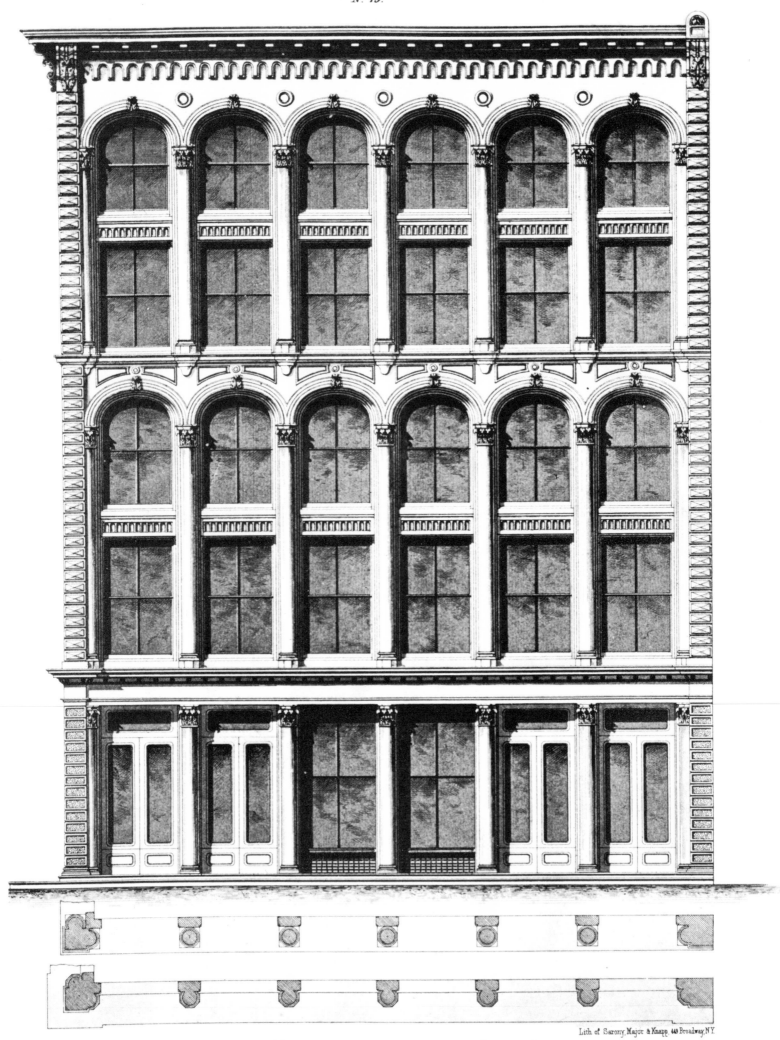

ARCHITECTURAL IRON WORKS, — NEW-YORK.